Corporate Acquisitions and Mergers in Belarus

Corporate Acquisitions and Mergers in Belarus

Second Edition

Helen Mourashko

Anna Solovei

Mikita Talkanitsa

Anna Protas

Larysa Kozhich

Valentina Belevich

Irina Golubich

Ulyana Bulhakava

Iryna Andryieuskaya

Viktoryia Semianitskaya

Valeryia Getsman

Revera

This book was originally published as a chapter in Corporate Acquisitions and Mergers.

General Editor: Peter Begg

Published by:
Kluwer Law International B.V.
PO Box 316
2400 AH Alphen aan den Rijn
The Netherlands
E-mail: lrs-sales@wolterskluwer.com
Website: www.wolterskluwer.com/en/solutions/kluwerlawinternational

Sold and distributed by:
Wolters Kluwer Legal & Regulatory U.S.
920 Links Avenue
Landisville, PA 17538
United States of America
E-mail: customer.service@wolterskluwer.com

DISCLAIMER: The material in this volume is in the nature of general comment only. It is not offered as advice on any particular matter and should not be taken as such. The editor and the contributing authors expressly disclaim all liability to any person with regard to anything done or omitted to be done, and with respect to the consequences of anything done or omitted to be done wholly or partly in reliance upon the whole or any part of the contents of this volume. No reader should act or refrain from acting on the basis of any matter contained in this volume without first obtaining professional advice regarding the particular facts and circumstances at issue. Any and all opinions expressed herein are those of the particular author and are not necessarily those of the editor or publisher of this volume.

Printed on acid-free paper

ISBN 978-94-035-1737-7

e-Book: ISBN 978-94-035-1747-6
web-PDF: ISBN 978-94-035-1757-5

Printed in the Netherlands.

Contents

Revera

Revera Belarus is the national leader and the largest legal firm in Belarus.

Our company has focused on development and growth since 1998 and regardless of circumstances, we have consistently grown in terms of volume of business.

Today we have over fifty specialist staff members, and our expertise comprises over eighty specialities, providing comprehensive support to our clients in any task of their business.

We have been listed as No. 1 in the international rankings of Chambers Global, LEGAL 500, IFLR 1 000.

Our clients are leaders in the Belarusian market, renowned personalities and international companies operating in Belarus.

Our method of operation can be characterised as a full-service boutique. Our strategy successfully combines the principles of a full-service legal firm, while concurrently creating a 'starry' highly tailored practice focusing on crucial business lines. This allows us to provide high-quality expertise and services for our clients in all matters of Belarusian business law.

Authors

The publication has been reviewed and coordinated by Anna Solovei, Counsel, Head of M&A and Corporate Structuring Technology Companies Practice of REVERA law group and Helen Mourashko, Partner of REVERA law group.

Helen Mourashko specialises in complex M&A transactions, transactions for attracting direct and venture capital investments in technology industries and also advises clients on a wide range of issues during complex cross-border projects in the field of corporate law, including corporate restructuring of groups of companies. Helen took part in the most significant transactions in the Information Technology (IT) sector of Belarus.

Helen participates in the development of Belarusian legislation in the field of IT, as well as in the development of the national startup ecosystem. She took part in the working group on the development of the revolutionary Decree No. 8, as well as in the development of other progressive legislative acts.

Anna Solovei specialises in supporting mergers and acquisitions in the IT sphere and restructuring of groups of companies with the participation of foreign entities. Moreover, Anna has solid experience in due diligence checks of IT companies and legal representation with respect to formalisation and protection of intellectual property rights.

Mikita Talkanitsa specialises in supporting mergers and acquisitions and restructuring of groups of companies. In addition, Mikita advises clients on antitrust issues. Mikita's portfolio of projects also includes legal support for companies in labour and migration law.

Anna Protas consults companies on taxation and application of double taxation treaties. Anna supports clients in matters involving pre-trial settlement of disputes relating to tax inspections.

Larysa Kozhich specialises in legal support of M&A deals and corporate restructuring of groups of companies. Larysa consults clients on antitrust law.

Valentina Belevich specialises in a wide range of corporate matters – from procedures for starting a Belarusian business, building relations between founders to legal due diligence of corporate activities and sale of businesses.

Irina Golubich works in the sphere of legal support of M&A deals, international business restructuring and selection of suitable jurisdictions for holdings, analysis of foreign jurisdictions in terms of corporate law, tax regulation, migration procedures, building interconnections and flows within the group of companies, preparation of contractual binding for companies and conducting legal due diligence.

Ulyana Bulhakava specialises in advising foreign and Belarusian companies on corporate law matters, including issues related to the incorporation of legal entities, the purchase of businesses and withdrawal from them, as well as on issues of attracting investment. Ulyana also has significant experience in a wide range of labour issues.

Iryna Andryieuskaya specialises in advising clients on various issues of corporate law as well as on issues of antitrust law.

Viktoryia Semianitskaya specialises in M&A transactions and restructuring of IT business with a foreign element, particularly on issues of transaction structuring, analysis of foreign jurisdictions for incorporation and doing business, and selection of instruments for protection of parties' interests. Viktoryia also takes part in legal due diligence and preparation of agreements in the sphere of intellectual property.

Valeryia Getsman specialises in corporate law and M&A matters, including investment raising, company formation, purchase and sale of businesses. Valeriya is also involved in employment law projects.

REVERA Belarus

belarus.revera.legal

8, Oboynaya str., 220004, Minsk, Belarus

Tel.: +375 44 500 15 10

E-mail: belarus@revera.legal

1 LOCAL ECONOMIC, POLITICAL AND CULTURAL ASPECTS

1.1 General Comments on the Country Profile

[01] Belarus is located on the eastern border of Europe and is positioned as a major trading route between Europe and the Commonwealth of Independent States (CIS). Belarus' unique location is of great importance for the development of trade, economic and humanitarian ties, and international tourism.

[02] Belarus has an area of 207 600 km² being the 84th largest country in the world. It borders Ukraine to the south, Russia to the east, Poland, Latvia, and Lithuania to the west and north-west.

[03] At the top level of administration, the territory of Belarus is divided into six regions and the city of Minsk, which has a special status as it is the capital of Belarus. At the second level, the regions are divided into districts. Apart from Minsk, there are other major cities such as Brest, Mogilev, Grodno, Gomel, and Vitebsk.

[04] Belarus has an extensive road and rail transport network of approximately 86 700 km of public highway network and 5 490 km of railways. In 2021, the state program Roads of Belarus 2021–2025 was approved with the aim to improve the transport and operational condition of public roads through increased investment in transport infrastructure to meet the needs of the economy and society in transport links.

[05] Natural resources of Belarus include potassium salts, wood, peat, granite, dolomite, limestone, clays, sand, minor oil and natural gas fields. Forests are among the country's key renewable natural resources. Belarus is among the ten 'forest states' of Europe.

[06] There are two official languages in Belarus: Russian and Belarusian. Most of the citizens speak Russian. Other languages such as Polish, Ukrainian and Hebrew are spoken within local communities.

[07] The official currency of Belarus is the Belarusian rouble (BYN).

[08] The population of Belarus as of 1 January 2022 is 9 255 524, a decline of 94 100 (1%) against 2021. The percentage of urban population is 78%. The majority of Belarusian citizens – 84.9% of the population – are ethnic Belarusians, followed by a sizeable minority of Russians (7.5%) as well as Poles, Ukrainians and others.

[09] According to the official statistics, in 2022, the employed population comprised 4 847 100. The employment rate of the population of Belarus (the ratio of the employed population to the population aged 15–74 years) in 2022 was 67.7%. The unemployment rate (according to the methodology of the International Labor Organization) is 3.6% of the workforce.

[10] Recent statistics indicate that the average wage in Belarus is BYN1 684.9, which is approximately USD670.

1.2 Government and Political System

[11] Belarus declared its independence on 25 August 1991. In 1994, the first president of Belarus Alexander Lukashenko was elected who remains in office so far.

[12] Belarus is a unitary parliamentary-presidential republic with state power divided among the legislative, executive and judicial branches of government.

[13] The government is implementing social and economic development program for 2021–2025 so that by 2025, Belarus will have entered the top thirty countries with the most comfortable conditions for doing business. The improvements cover administrative procedures, taxation, pricing, licensing, preferential treatment for investors and protection of their rights.

[14] Belarus is welcoming to foreign investors, although many areas of the economy tend to be dominated by state companies. In 2022, foreign investors invested USD7 bn in the real sector of the Belarusian economy. The main investors in Belarusian organisations were business entities from Russia (56.1% of all investments received), Cyprus (14.7%), the Netherlands (4.1%) and Ukraine (2.9%). Foreign direct investment totalled USD6 bn or 85.4% of all incoming foreign injections. In 2022, Belarusian entities sent investments worth USD6.3 bn abroad. Of these investments 87% were transferred to business entities in Russia, but also to Ireland (2.4%) and Kazakhstan (1.6%).

[15] Belarus has been a member of the Eurasian Economic Union (EAEU) since 1 January 2015. Belarus has been in the accession process to the World Trade Organization (WTO) since 1993.

[16] Belarus has signed bilateral agreements on free trade with Armenia, Azerbaijan, Kazakhstan, Kyrgyzstan, Moldova, Russia, Serbia, Tajikistan, Turkmenistan, Ukraine, and Uzbekistan.

[17] Belarus is also a party to the CIS Agreement on the Establishment of a Free Trade Area signed on 15 April 1994 (with amendments of 2 April 1999). The Agreement is applied to relations with the Member States for which the CIS Treaty on Free Trade Area of 18 October 2011 did not enter into force, in particular, with Azerbaijan. Belarus and Georgia agreed to apply the Agreement on the Establishment of a Free Trade Area in mutual trade after Georgia's withdrawal from the CIS.

[18] The Free Trade Agreement between the EAEU and its Member States, on the one part, and Vietnam, on the other part, entered into force on 5 October 2016 and provides for significant reduction or abolition of import duties on almost all key positions of Belarusian exports to Vietnam.

[19] On 25 October 2019, the Agreement on Economic and Trade Cooperation between the EAEU and its Member States, on the one part, and China, on the other part, entered into force. Also on 27 October 2019, an Interim Agreement leading to the formation of a free trade area between the EAEU and its Member States, on the one part, and Iran, on the other part, entered into force. Under the

Protocol on the extension of the Interim Agreement entered into force on 25 October 2022, the duration of the Interim Agreement has been extended until 27 October 2025, or until the free trade agreement stipulated in the Interim Agreement becomes effective, whichever happens first.

[20] In 2019, the EAEU Member States completed negotiations on the conclusion of free trade agreements with Singapore and Serbia. The Free Trade Agreement between the Eurasian Economic Union and its Member States, of the one part, and the Republic of Serbia, of the other part, entered into force on 10 July 2021. Negotiations on concluding free trade area agreement with Egypt are underway. In 2022, the leaders of the EAEU Member States launched free trade agreement negotiations with Indonesia and the UAE in accordance with Joint Feasibility Study Reports.

[21] In 2022, the Government of Belarus imposed restrictions on foreign shareholders of Belarusian legal entities who do not have the right to sell their shares in the share capital. In early 2023, the laws 'On seizure of property' and 'On questions of placement under temporary external management' were adopted, which introduced restrictions to businesses with foreign investments.

1.3 Legal System

[22] The legal system of Belarus was historically formed in the conditions of the legal culture of continental Europe. It belongs to the so-called family of Romano-Germanic law which is characterised by a fairly clear structure dividing it into branches and institutions. There is no system of judicial precedent in Belarus. Only written legislative enactments are considered binding on all, although in practice judges do tend to follow previous judicial decisions.

1.4 Current Economic Aspects

[23] The Belarusian economy is based on the socially oriented economic model. Centralised distribution and planning are used in terms of macroeconomic indices only. The Belarusian economy has a high degree of openness and is oriented to foreign markets. More than 60% of manufactured goods are exported. In 2022, the country's foreign trade turnover amounted to USD89 220 m. Exports amounted to USD46 767m, and imports – USD42 453 m.

[24] In 2022, Belarus exported its products to 161 countries. The most important export positions are products of petrochemistry, mechanical engineering, metallurgy, woodworking, light industry, dairy and meat products, furniture, glass, fibreglass, and cement. The main imports are energy resources (oil and natural gas), raw materials, materials and components (metals and products from them, raw materials for chemical production, machine parts), and technological equipment.

[25] In 2022, export of Belarusian services amounted to USD9.2 bn, which is 10.8% less than in 2021. The main exported services were transportation services and Information Technology (IT) services. Next places are held by tourist services, construction services, advertising/marketing/exhibition services, computer services and financial services. Imports of services decreased by 11.3% compared to 2021 to USD5 bn.

[26] The inflow of foreign investments into the economy of Belarus by the end of 2022 amounted to USD6.98 bn, a 19.8% decrease compared to 2021. The most attractive economic activities for direct investment were industry (USD0.66 bn or 43.2% of the total), wholesale and retail trade, car repair (USD0.22 bn or 14.2%), financial and insurance activities (USD0.17 bn or 11.3%); construction (USD0.15 bn or 9.5%).

[27] Belarus is dependent on energy supplies (mainly from Russia) and also suffers from high inflation by European standards.

[28] In 2022, the number of publicly disclosed transactions carried out with the participation of residents of Belarus decreased to 30, i.e., by 57% compared to 2021. The IT sector is the leading sector in terms of M&A. Other transactions were concluded in sectors of the economy such as telecommunications, e-commerce, trade, engineering and agriculture, light industry, hotel business, pharmaceuticals, sale of petroleum products and finance.

1.5 Main Industries

[29] The country's major industries include energy production, machine engineering, agriculture, the chemical industry, forestry, the construction industry and production of construction materials, and the extractive industry. In 2022, gross domestic product (GDP) amounted to USD68.9 bn (a 4.7% decrease in comparison to 2021). The growth rate of the real disposable income decreased by 3.6% compared to 2021. In the total amount of income, wages accounted for 64.8%, income from entrepreneurial and other income-generating activities – 8.2%, social payments to the population (pensions, scholarships and other payments) – 22.2%, income from property and other income – 4.8%.

[30] Belarus deserves special mention with regard to its IT sector. As a part of the global IT business, the Belarusian software services sector has been developing at a rapid pace. The country's reputation for scientific and IT excellence, complemented by a competitive labour market, has attracted the interest of numerous IT-intensive companies.

[31] In 2005, the High-Tech Park (HTP) was established in the country – a special tax and legal regime that made life easier for Belarusian IT projects and attracted foreign corporations. As of 1 January 2023, 1 065 companies are HTP residents and are engaged in the development of software products, providing IT services to customers from around the world.

1.6 Cultural Aspects

[32] Belarus is open for business. This fact can be evidenced by a developing market, a qualified and hard-working labour force, low salaries and taxes, a highly developed IT industry, and visa-free.

[33] As a general matter, Belarus is not a particularly expensive place to do business. Minsk, the capital, is the most expensive city in the country.

[34] The national features of Belarusians are openness and trust in people. Therefore, in business, Belarusians tend to scrupulously observe agreements and carefully protect their reputation. Belarusians believe that a successful business can be built only on the basis of trust gained through good personal relationships.

[35] Any business meeting should be planned and agreed upon in advance and confirmed again immediately before the meeting. The first business contacts imply a business environment and a business style of communication and clothing.

[36] Negotiations can take a long time, since in Belarus, it is customary to coordinate any point of the contract with the higher management.

2 THE REGULATORY FRAMEWORK

2.1 Business Vehicles

[37] There are no specific requirements for foreigners who wish to start a business in Belarus. Investors, whether they are residents of Belarus or of any other country, are entitled to the same legal treatment and equal rights as Belarusian citizens for incorporating a business in Belarus. In order to incorporate a legal entity, an applicant must pass through a number of legal formalities, including registration in the Uniform State Register of Legal Entities and Individual Entrepreneurs. A legal entity is required to have its own name, statutory fund (to be formed, unless otherwise stipulated by law, within one year from the date of state registration – there being a minimum amount stipulated by law for certain forms of business), management bodies, registered office and bank account(s). Legal entities registered in Belarus are subject to Belarusian law. However, agreements concluded by Belarusian companies with foreign companies may be governed by any law chosen by the parties.

[38] Belarusian legislation provides for the following legal forms of business entity:

- Individual Entrepreneur (abbreviated as IE).
- Farm Enterprise (peasant economy) (abbreviated as FE).
- Unitary Enterprise (abbreviated as UE).
- Production Cooperative (abbreviated as PC).
- General Partnership (abbreviated as GP).

- Special Partnership (abbreviated as SP).
- Additional Liability Company (abbreviated as ALC).
- Limited Liability Company (abbreviated as LLC).
- Open/Public Joint-stock Company (abbreviated as OJSC or PJSC).
- Closed Joint-stock Company (abbreviated as CJSC).

[39] Business entities may also establish representative offices and branch offices. Branch offices may only be created by legal entities – residents of Belarus. Representative offices, which are not allowed to carry out business activities, can be established by foreign companies.

[40] Most businesses in Belarus are legal entities organised in the form of an LLC, or a CJSC and OJSC, as these offer the most favourable legal terms, less often in the form of a UE and ALC. Only citizens of Belarus and foreigners having a resident card in Belarus are entitled to be registered as IEs.

2.1.1 Unitary Enterprise

[41] A UE is a commercial entity having no right of ownership to property allocated to it. The enterprise founder or the person/entity that purchased or otherwise acquired title thereto is the owner of its property. Only one individual or one legal entity can be the founder (and the property holder) of a UE. For a UE set up by an individual, the word 'private' must be used in its name. Property of a UE cannot be divided into contributions (shares, equity interests) and cannot be divided among employees. The charter is the founding document of any UE.

[42] A manager (director) appointed by the owner is the managerial body of a UE. The owner of a UE may also act as its director. Powers of the director of a UE may be delegated contractually to another commercial entity (management company) or to an IE (executive manager) by the owner's decision.

[43] The legislation does not stipulate a minimum amount of statutory fund for UEs. The owner determines the amount of the statutory fund independently.

[44] A UE is liable for its obligations with all of the property belonging to it and is not liable for obligations of its founder. Subsidiary liability for enterprise obligations will be imposed on the owner only if the owner's actions have caused economic insolvency (bankruptcy) of an enterprise.

2.1.2 Limited Liability Company

[45] An LLC is a business entity with a number of participants not more than fifty, having a statutory fund divided into shares of certain sizes as specified by its constituent documents. A single founder (either an individual or a legal entity) may also form an LLC.

[46] The legislation does not stipulate a minimum amount of statutory fund for an LLC. The founders determine the amount of the statutory fund independently.

[47] The charter duly approved by the founders is the constitutional document of an LLC.

[48] An LLC is liable for its obligations with all of the property belonging to it. An LLC is not liable for obligations of its participants, except in specific cases provided for by the legislative acts or its charter. Participants of an LLC are not liable for their obligations and will only bear the risks of losses pertaining to company activities to the extent of the value of their contributions to the company's statutory fund. Those participants of an LLC who have made their contributions otherwise than in full will be jointly and severally liable for the company's obligations to the extent of the unpaid part of each such participant's contribution.

[49] The corporate structure of an LLC comprises the following.

General Meeting of Shareholders

[50] The General Meeting of Shareholders is the supreme authority of an LLC that takes the most important decisions on company activities. If an LLC consists only of one participant, the General Meeting of Shareholders will not be held and the sole participant will exercise the authority of the General Meeting of Shareholders.

Board of Directors or Supervisors

[51] The Board of Directors (Supervisory Board) will be formed where its formation is stipulated by the company charter.

Executive Body: Sole Director or Administrative Board

[52] Powers of the executive body may be executed by the Sole Director and (or) by the Administrative Board or delegated contractually to another commercial entity (management company) or to an IE (executive manager) by the decision of the General Meeting of Shareholders.

[53] The director or a person heading a collegial executive body (Administrative Board), acting within their competence, without a power of attorney, can act on behalf of the company, including representing its interests and concluding transactions on its behalf. The power of the Executive Body may be restricted by the company charter.

Inspector or Inspection Commission: LLC's Controlling Authority

[54] Inspector or Inspection Commission carries out internal control of financial and economic activities of the company. Internal control is carried out in the form of revisions in all or several areas of the company's activities and inspections in one or more related areas or for a certain period of the company's activities by its branches and representative offices.

[55] The Board of Directors (Supervisory Board), Executive Body and Inspection Commission are accountable to the General Meeting of Shareholders or, in case of a company consisting of a sole participant, to such sole participant.

2.1.3 Additional Liability Company

[56] An ALC is a company with a number of participants not more than fifty, having a statutory fund divided into shares of certain sizes as specified by its constituent documents. Additional liability companies are governed by the same rules and regulations as established by the legislation for limited liability companies (with regard to constituent documents, number of participants, size of statutory fund, corporate structure, etc.).

[57] The only difference between an ALC and an LLC is that participants of the former will jointly and severally bear subsidiary responsibility for any company obligations with their property to the extent determined by the company charter, but not less than the amount established by the legislative acts, in proportion to participants' contributions to the statutory fund of such ALC. The charter of an ALC may establish a different procedure for the distribution of additional responsibility among its participants.

[58] At present, the minimum size of subsidiary responsibility in case of an ALC is equivalent to at least fifty basic units.

2.1.4 Closed Joint-Stock Company

[59] To date the number of participants in a CJSC is unlimited (there used to be a restriction of no more than fifty participants). But the restrictions on the number of participants may be established by the company charter.

[60] The minimum amount of the statutory fund of a CJSC is one hundred basic units. The statutory fund is divided into a number of shares of equal nominal value.

[61] The charter is the constituent document of a CJSC.

[62] The corporate structure of a CJSC comprises the same elements as the corporate structure of an LLC. However, formation of the Board of Directors (Supervisory Board) of an CJSC is mandatory as required by law, if the number of its shareholders is more than fifty. In a CJSC, the number of shareholders – owners of voting shares of which is more than one hundred, a counting commission is created.

[63] Shareholders are not liable for company obligations and will only bear the risks of losses pertaining to company activities to the extent of the value of their shares.

[64] A CJSC is not entitled to carry out public subscriptions for capital stock issued by it or in any other way offer capital stock for purchase by the general public.

2.1.5 Open Joint-Stock Company

[65] The number of participants in an OJSC is unlimited.

[66] The minimum amount of the statutory fund of an OJSC is 400 basic units. The statutory fund is divided into a number of shares of equal nominal value.

[67] The charter is the constituent document of an OJSC.

[68] The corporate structure of an OJSC comprises the same elements as the corporate structure of an LLC. However, formation of the Board of Directors (Supervisory Board) of an OJSC is mandatory as required by law, if the number of its shareholders is more than fifty. Also, the Controlling Authority in the OJSC must be specifically the Inspection Commission (but not the Inspector at the option of the shareholders as in LLC). In an OJSC, the number of shareholders – owners of voting shares of which is more than one hundred, a counting commission is created.

[69] Shareholders are not liable for the obligations of an OJSC and will only bear the risks of losses pertaining to company activities to the extent of the value of their shares.

[70] A shareholder may dispose of his shares to the general public without consent from other shareholders (with some exceptions, where a regional executive committee (or Minsk municipal committee) has a preemptive right to acquire ownership of stock of certain OJSCs).

[71] An OJSC is entitled to carry out public subscriptions for shares issued by it or public sales of additional shares in a manner and upon terms prescribed by applicable laws on securities. An OJSC is also entitled to a private offering of additional shares where such additional shares are being placed at the cost of company capital and/or at the cost of shareholders' funds, and in other cases stipulated by legal acts.

2.1.6 Representative Offices and Branches of Business Entities

[72] A representative office is a subdivision of a foreign corporate entity located within the territory of Belarus, safeguarding and representing the interests of such foreign entity and exercising other functions in accordance with legislation. The representative office of a foreign corporate entity cannot carry out business activities.

[73] A branch is a subdivision of a corporate entity located outside its main premises and exercising all or some of its functions, including representation functions.

[74] Representative offices and branches are not deemed to be 'legal entities' and they may only operate on behalf of the legal entity which created them. A representative or a branch manager must act under a power of attorney. Property of representative offices and branches must be accounted for separately on the balance sheets of the founding legal entities.

[75] Belarusian legislation does not allow foreign legal entities to establish branches; therefore, foreign entities may only establish standalone structural subdivisions in the form of representative offices in Belarus.

[76] The procedure for conducting business through a representation office is described in detail in section 2.1.7 below.

2.1.7 Ways of Doing Business for Foreign Entities
and Individuals in Belarus

[77] Foreign investors can choose between the two following ways of doing business in Belarus:

(1) establishment of a Belarusian legal entity in one of the above-listed forms. The statutory fund of a commercial entity must be declared in BYN. Foreign investors are entitled to make contributions to the statutory fund in foreign currency, but at the point of declaring the statutory fund in the corporate documents such contributions must be recalculated in BYN at the official rate stated on the date of their actual transfer;
(2) doing business via a permanent representative office within the territory of Belarus.

Doing Business via a Permanent Representative Office in Belarus

[78] Doing business via a permanent representative office in Belarus, according to the Tax Code of Belarus, means doing business by virtue of:
 – a permanent establishment through which a foreign entity is eligible to carry on, either fully or partially, entrepreneurial or other activities in Belarus;
 – a dependent agent (a corporate entity or an individual, operating in the name of or on behalf of a foreign entity and/or having/using the foreign entity's powers to conclude contracts or negotiate essential terms thereof).

Carrying Out Activities via a Permanent Establishment in Belarus

[79] A foreign company must be registered with the local tax authorities according to the location of its permanent establishment in Belarus.

[80] The legislation of Belarus prescribes certain periods of legal validity for permanent establishments of foreign entities. However, if an international treaty to which Belarus is a party prescribes other terms, then the norms of that international treaty shall prevail.

[81] As a general rule, a place of work/service delivery will be acknowledged as a 'permanent establishment' under the legislation of Belarus where the relevant activities are carried out (either continuously or in total) for 180 days or more in any twelve-month period starting or finishing in a respective tax period.

[82] Similar norms apply to construction sites and installation sites (assembly objects) that are acknowledged as a permanent establishment of a foreign entity, where such site/object is located within the territory of Belarus for 180 days or more in any twelve-month period starting or finishing in a relevant tax period.

[83] A 'construction site', 'installation object' or 'assembly object' of a foreign entity in Belarus is a site used for the construction of new products/objects, the reconstruction (modernisation), expansion, re-engineering and/or repair of existing real estate objects (except for aircraft and ships, inland waterways craft and

space objects), or a site used for the construction and/or installation, repair and reconstruction (modernisation), expansion and/or re-engineering of structures, machinery and equipment, which requires a rigid attachment to the footing or to the structural component(s) of capital structures/buildings.

[84] In defining the period of existence of a construction site or an installation/ assembly object, the following time frames are not included:

– time needed for design of the object by a foreign entity outside Belarus;
– time spent by the contractor on other construction sites and/or objects not related to the construction site/object.

Doing Business via a Dependent Agent

[85] A foreign entity may operate in Belarus via a dependent agent – a Belarusian corporate entity or an IE.

[86] A 'dependent agent' is a legal entity or an individual operating in the name of or on behalf of a foreign entity and/or which is authorised to conclude contracts or negotiate essential terms of contracts.

[87] According to the Tax Code of Belarus, doing business via a dependent agent is recognised as operating via a permanent representative office for the purposes of taxation. Therefore, a foreign entity operating via a dependent agent is obliged to pay taxes on profits derived in Belarus. Taxes of such foreign entity must be paid by the agent according to the place of its tax registration.

[88] If an agent operates within the framework of its ordinary course of business (i.e., as an independent agent or an agent with independent status), it is not recognised as a permanent representative office for the purposes of taxation. 'Ordinary course of business' means operating independently without instructions and/or control by such foreign entity and bearing the business risks of its own operations (not borne by the foreign entity which it represents). In such cases, the foreign entity will not pay the profit tax, but it will pay tax on income from any activities carried out via a permanent representative office.

[89] According to Belarusian law, business entities have to obtain special permits (licences) in order to carry out certain types of activities. As a result of this rule, agents cannot carry out activities subject to licensing.

[90] Belarusian legislation provides that a clause stipulating exclusivity of the relationship cannot be introduced into an agency contract involving a Belarusian party. Any clause requiring refusal to contract with other suppliers or purchasers contradicts the Belarusian antimonopoly legislation and may be invalidated under Belarusian law.

Establishing a Representative Office in Belarus

[91] Any foreign entity may establish its representative office in Belarus. This does not imply any entrepreneurial activity in Belarus and, as a general rule, is needed exclusively for the performance of representative functions and/or preparation for doing business in Belarus. However, if any attributes of a permanent representative

office are found in the activities of a foreign entity for taxation purposes (execution of works, rendering of services, selling goods, pursuant to the above-mentioned requirements), such foreign entity will pay taxes in Belarus under the rules applying to entrepreneurial activities via a permanent representative office.

[92] Representative offices of foreign entities are established and managed in Belarus on the basis of permits issued by the relevant local regional executive committee (or Minsk municipal committee) depending on the location of such representative office.

[93] A representative office:

– is not recognised as a legal entity by Belarusian law;
– is not entitled to carry on entrepreneurial activities.

[94] A representative office of a foreign non-commercial entity can only be opened to implement, on behalf of such foreign entity:

(1) social support and protection of citizens, including improvement of the material standing of the poor, social rehabilitation of the unemployed, the disabled and other persons who due to their physical or mental state or other circumstances are not able to exercise their rights and legitimate interests;
(2) preparation/training of citizens for the prevention of accidents, industrial accidents, man-made dangerous situations, natural hazards, natural or other disasters, social, ethnic and religious conflicts, provision of support in dealing with consequences thereof, as well as to the victims of repression, refugees and internally displaced persons;
(3) contribution to promoting:
    (a) peace, friendship and harmony among nations, prevention of social, ethnic and religious conflicts;
    (b) strengthening the prestige of the family in society;
    (c) protection of motherhood, fatherhood and childhood;
    (d) activities in the field of education, science, culture, art, education and personal development;
    (e) activities in the field of preventive health care and public health protection, promotion of healthy lifestyle, and improving the moral and psychological condition of citizens;
    (f) activities in the field of physical culture and sports;
    (g) environmental and animal protection;
    (h) protection and maintenance of buildings, structures, and other objects and areas of historical, cultural, religious or environmental value, and burial places.
(4) other socially useful activities.

[95] Representative offices of foreign educational organisations may be opened in order to promote international cooperation in the field of education, including the conclusion of agreements on cooperation between educational institutions of Belarus and foreign educational organisations, to study best practices of the

Belarusian education system, to facilitate the exchange of experience and information in the field of education and science, and realisation of advertising and information arrangements relating to educational activities of foreign educational organisations.

[96] A representative office of a foreign commercial entity may be opened, unless otherwise stipulated by international treaties or legislative acts of Belarus, only for the purposes of preparatory and auxiliary activities on behalf of such foreign entity, including:

- assistance in implementing international treaties of Belarus on cooperation in economy, trade, finance, science and technology, transport, or seeking opportunities for the further development and improvement of such cooperation, arranging and expanding the exchange of economic, commercial, scientific and technical information;
- researching the commodities/services market of Belarus;
- exploring opportunities for investment in Belarus;
- creating commercial entities with the participation of foreign investors;
- selling/booking tickets for aircraft, rail, road and sea transport;
- other socially useful activities.

[97] By 31 March each year, companies are obliged to prepare annual financial statements for the previous financial year, i.e., for the period ended 31 December of the previous calendar year. A company's annual financial statements are signed by its chief accountant and managing director. The annual financial statements comprise the balance sheet, income statement, cash-flow statement, statement of changes in equity and accompanying notes. Certain types of companies (for instance, joint-stock companies) are obliged to conduct an audit with respect to their financial statements. Mandatory audit of the annual accounting (financial) statements must be carried out by no later than 30 June of the year following the relevant reporting year. Following the preparation of the annual financial statements, the sole shareholder or the general meeting of the shareholders approves the annual financial statements by virtue of a resolution. By virtue of the same resolution, the main corporate body may also decide on the profit distribution. Companies are obliged to submit annual individual financial statements prepared not later than 31 March of the year following the reporting year to the tax authority at the place of registration.

[98] Companies are obliged to make changes to their charters within two months and to submit them for state registration in the event of a change in the name, a change of the owner or a change in the composition of participants. In the event of a change in the location, or the appointment (replacement) of the head of a company, the company must, within ten working days, send a notification to the registering authority in the form established by the Ministry of Justice.

[99] Joint-stock companies are also required to disclose certain information (e.g., on transactions with affiliates, on major transactions) on a single information resource of the securities market and place such information on their official website (if they have one).

2.2 Laws Affecting M&A

[100] The main laws concerning M&A activity in Belarus are the following:

- Civil Code of Belarus dated 7 December 1998 No. 218-Z.
- Law of Belarus dated 9 December 1992 No. 2020-XII 'On Companies'.
- Law of Belarus dated 19 January 1993 No. 2103-XII 'On privatization of state property and reorganisation of state unitary enterprises into open joint-stock companies' regulating the issues of transformation of state UEs into OJSCs.
- Decree of the President of Belarus dated 16 January 2009 No. 1 'On State Registration and Liquidation (termination of activities) of Business Entities'.
- Law of Belarus dated 5 January 2015 No. 231-Z 'On the Securities Market'.
- Law of Belarus dated 12 December 2013 No. 94-Z 'On Counteracting Monopolistic Activities and Development of Competition'.
- Decree of the President of Belarus dated 21 December 2017 No. 8 'On the Development of the Digital Economy' (Decree No. 8).
- Edict of the President of Belarus dated 14 March 2022 No. 93 'On additional measures for ensuring the stable functioning of economic'.
- Resolution of Council of Ministers dated 1 July 2022 No. 436 'On the list of persons'.

[101] Reorganisation of a company may be carried out in the form of consolidation, merger, division, separation or transformation.

[102] *Consolidation* is the creation of a new business entity by transferring, to a new business entity created as a result of the consolidation, all rights and obligations of the business entities participating in the consolidation, with the termination of their activities. Companies participating in the consolidation conclude a consolidation agreement, which determines the procedure and conditions for the consolidation.

[103] *Merger* with a business entity is the termination of the activities of the merged business entity with the transfer of its rights and obligations to the business entity into which the merger is being carried out. The merged business entity and the business entity into which the merger is carried out conclude a merger agreement, which determines the procedure and conditions for the merger.

[104] *Division* of a business entity is the termination of its activities with the transfer of its rights and obligations to the newly formed business entities. The general meeting of shareholders of the company decides on the reorganisation and determines its procedure and conditions.

[105] *Separation* from a business entity is the creation of one or more new business entities with the partial transfer to them of the rights and obligations of the reorganised business entity without termination of its activities. The general meeting of shareholders of the company decides on the reorganisation and determines its procedure and conditions.

[106] A business entity of one form may be *transformed* into a business entity of another form, a business partnership or a PC, as well as into a UE in the event only one participant remains in the company.

[107] Any reorganisations as well as any alienation of shares/stocks are restricted with respect to some business entities with foreign shareholders under the Edict of the President of the Republic of Belarus dated 14 March 2022 No. 93. The list of such business entities and their foreign shareholders is envisaged by Resolution of Council of Ministers dated 1 July 2022 No. 436.

[108] Business entity is obliged to notify in writing its creditors about the decision on reorganisation. The creditor of the business entity has the right to demand a prior termination or a prior performance of the obligations and compensation for losses.

[109] Companies have the right to regulate the labour discipline of employees by adoption of local legal acts which are considered to be one of the sources of regulation of labour: collective agreements, internal labour regulations and other local legal acts. Other local legal acts may, in particular, include:

– job (work) instructions;
– instructions on labour protection;
– regulations on remuneration;
– orders of the head of the company.

[110] Local legal acts are adopted in all organisations. The employer is obliged to acquaint employees with the current and new local legal acts that directly relate to the employees' labour functions. When organising the work of employees, the employer is obliged to ensure compliance with the conditions established in the local legal acts. Local legal acts may contain additional labour and other guarantees for employees in comparison with labour legislation. Both employee and employer are obliged to comply with the requirements of the local legal acts. In case of violation of the local legal acts by an employee, disciplinary measures may be applied to them.

[111] The list of local legal acts contained in the Labour Code is open. This means that companies may also adopt other local legal acts. However, local legal acts which are adopted by the employer are invalid if provisions of such acts are making the position of employees worse in comparison with the labour legislation.

2.3 Relevant Regulatory Authorities

[112] The main regulatory authority relevant to M&A activity is the Ministry of Antimonopoly Regulation and Trade of Belarus (for more information please *see* section 3.1).

[113] Another regulatory authority is the Belarusian Currency and Stock Exchange. The subject of its activity is the organisation of exchange trading in financial assets, including currency values and equity securities, with the exception of shares of CJSCs.

[114] After the conclusion of the share purchase agreement, it is necessary for CJSCs to register the agreement with the depositary. Furthermore, the buyer of a large block of shares in a CJSC is obliged to disclose information about such acquisition to the Securities Department of the Ministry of Finance (for more information please *see* section 2.6.7).

[115] Finally, there are state registration authorities responsible for registration of companies and changes in their statutory documents. State registration is carried out by the following registration authorities:

- the National Bank of the Republic of Belarus (hereinafter – NB) – banks and non-bank credit and financial organisations, including those located in Free Economic Zones (FEZ) and the Great Stone Chinese-Belarusian Industrial Park (Great Stone Industrial Park);
- the Ministry of Finance – insurance organisations, insurance brokers, associations of insurers, including those located in FEZ and the Great Stone Industrial Park;
- the Ministry of Justice – Chambers of Commerce and Industry;
- administrations of FEZ – companies in FEZ;
- the administration of the Great Stone Industrial Park – companies located on the territory of the Great Stone Industrial Park;
- regional executive committees and the Minsk City Executive Committee – other companies with the participation of foreign and international organisations;
- regional executive committees, Brest, Vitebsk, Gomel, Grodno, Minsk, Mogilev city executive committees – other companies. Regional executive committees have the right to delegate part of their powers for state registration to other local executive and administrative bodies, and city executive committees – to the corresponding district administrations in cities.

As a general rule, the decision on registration or on refusal is made on the day of submission of documents.

[116] Business entities are entitled to engage all aforementioned authorities directly without any local legal advisors. However, it is recommended to consult advisers at least when drawing up documents, applicants are responsible for complying with legal requirements when submitting the documents.

2.4 Controls/Restrictions on Foreign Investment

[117] As a general rule, Belarusian legislation allows foreign investors to carry out business activities on the same basis and with the same level of protection as domestic investors.

[118] To be functioning, a company must comply with the statutory requirements regarding permitting and licensing procedures. Although no special permit for a foreign investor to start a business in Belarus is required, there are numerous permits and licences which are mandatory for both a Belarusian and foreign company depending upon its contemplated area of activity.

[119] Belarusian legislation sets out two categories of restrictions applicable to investment activity in Belarus: (i) general restrictions relating to both domestic and foreign investors which envisage that certain types of activities must be carried out only by state-owned companies (e.g., armaments); and (ii) specific restrictions applicable to foreign investors.

[120] The following restrictions are applied to foreign investment:

No.	Economy Sector	Statutory Restrictions
1	Land transactions	Land plots, including those transferred in case of sale of state-owned real property, are granted to foreign entities only on a leasehold basis. A land plot may be privately owned by a foreign individual or a stateless person on grounds of inheritance, where he/she inherits a land plot or real estate on a land plot privately owned by testator, or on grounds of common joint property of spouses when a spouse is a citizen of Belarus unless otherwise stipulated by applicable legislative acts.
2	Privatisation	Property units owned exclusively by the state may not be privatised unless otherwise stipulated by applicable legislation or acts of the President of Belarus.
3	Insurance and other financial activities	A quota was established for foreign investors' participation in statutory funds of all insurance entities in Belarus – 30%.
4	Bank sector	A quota was established for foreign capital participation in the banking system of Belarus – 50% at most.
5	Activities of information agencies	Foreign legal entities, as well as foreign individuals and stateless persons having no permanent residence in Belarus, may establish mass media only jointly with citizens and/or legal entities of Belarus.
		A mass medium may not be edited by a commercial entity with at least 20% of participatory shares owned, jointly or individually, by a foreign state, foreign and/or international legal entity (or unincorporated entity), foreign individual or stateless person.

No.	Economy Sector	Statutory Restrictions
		A mass medium may not be edited by a non-commercial entity with at least 20% of its founders/participants being represented by a foreign state, foreign and/or international legal entity (or unincorporated entity), foreign individual or stateless person.
		Only citizens of Belarus may perform functions of chief editors of mass media.
6	Alcohol production	Production of cognacs, brandies and cognac-like liquors may only be carried out by state-owned legal entities or non-state legal entities with more than 30% of statutory fund owned by the state unless otherwise prescribed by the President of Belarus.

[121] The management bodies of a company, the shares of which belong to Belarus or to administrative-territorial units, shall include a representative (representatives) of the state. Moreover, under the Law of Belarus dated 3 January 2023 'On issues of transfer to interim external administration' private business entities with foreign shareholders can be transferred to interim external administration by the decision of regional executive committees and the Minsk City Executive Committee. This may happen if there is a risk of unreasonable termination of its activity or causing damage to the workforce (e.g., the CEO or shareholders make a decision which leads to termination of activity of the business entity). The list of business entities, which can be transferred to interim external administration is approved by committees.

[122] In general, the executive body of a company shall be located in Belarus. Companies may attract to Belarus and hire a foreigner as a director (for more information please *see* section 5.5). A foreigner may also be a member of the Board of Directors (Supervisory Board).

2.5 Incentives for Foreign Investment

[123] Relations pertaining to investment activities are regulated by the Law of Belarus 'On Investments' dated 12 July 2013, regulatory legal acts of the President, other legislation and international treaties of Belarus.

[124] In accordance with the Law of Belarus 'On Investments', 'investment' is property and/or other objects of civil law rights which belong to an investor on the basis of the ownership right (or another legal basis), and which the investor invests in the territory of Belarus in order to gain profit (income) and/or to achieve other specific socio-economic results or for other purposes not connected with personal, family, home and other similar usage, in the form of:

- monetary funds, including borrowed funds (including loans and credits), stocks, other movable and immovable property;
- rights of claim duly assessed (in monetary terms); participatory shares, property shares in commercial entities established within the territory of Belarus;
- other objects of civil rights duly assessed, except for certain types of objects of civil rights withdrawn from public circulation.

[125] Investment activities in Belarus may be carried out by any means complying with Belarusian laws. The Law of Belarus 'On Investments' specifies, in particular, the following ways of engaging in investment activities:

- creation of a commercial entity;
- acquisition, creation (including by means of construction) of real estate units, except for cases when living quarters/spaces are purchased or constructed by Belarusian citizens, foreign citizens or stateless persons, for permanent accommodation of such persons and/or their families;
- acquisition of intellectual property rights;
- acquisition of capital stock, participatory shares, or shares of stock in a commercial entity, in particular, by means of increasing its authorised capital;
- under a concession agreement;
- within the framework of public-private partnership;
- other ways of complying with the Belarusian legislation.

2.5.1 External Safeguards of Investments in Belarus

[126] In order to create conditions corresponding to international standards of insuring foreign investors' risks, and in order to attract foreign financial resources without providing guarantees of the Government of Belarus to foreign investors and, correspondingly, without increase of the national external debt, the Government facilitated full-fledged membership of Belarus in the Multilateral Investment Guarantee Agency (hereinafter – MIGA).

[127] Belarus joined the MIGA Convention in December 1992, ratified the amendments to the Convention in 2011, and signed and ratified the Agreement on the legal protection of guaranteed foreign investments and the Agreement on local currency use in 2011–2012.

[128] MIGA is an organisation of the World Bank Group and therefore allows investors to insure their current projects against political and non-commercial risks (restrictions of currency transfer and exchange, expropriation, war, civil disorders and other risks).

[129] All projects have to comply with the development goals of the host country and the MIGA sustainable development policies.

[130] Safeguards for investors' rights and protection of investments have been provided for by a number of international agreements. A unique position among them is held by Appendix 16 to the Treaty on the EAEU endorsing the Protocol on

trade in services and investment activities. This Protocol provides for the following guarantees:

- equitable and peer treatment of investments and investment activities carried out by investors of other Member States;
- application of the national regime to investors of other Member States;
- granting most-favoured-nation status to investors of other Member States;
- repatriation of incomes;
- indemnity for losses;
- prompt and adequate compensation in case of expropriation;
- subrogation of investors' rights to a Member State;
- each investor facing a dispute is free to choose between proceeding in the recipient country or ad hoc arbitration by the chamber of commerce under the United Nations Commission on International Trade Law (UNCITRAL) or International Centre for Settlement of Investment Disputes (ICSID) rules.

[131] At the same time, the EAEU Agreement provides that Member States may restrict the activities of investors from other Member States, or introduce exemptions from national regimes, which still hinders the formation of a single investment environment.

[132] Belarus is a party to the fundamental international conventions on investment regulation such as:

- The Convention on the Settlement of Investment Disputes Between States and Nationals of Other States (1965).
- The Convention on the Recognition and Enforcement of Foreign Arbitral Awards (1958).
- The Seoul Convention Establishing the MIGA (1985).

[133] In order to create favourable conditions for investments made by foreign investors and to promote mutual assistance in the realisation and protection of such investments, Belarus has signed over sixty bilateral agreements on the encouragement and mutual protection of investments and over sixty bilateral agreements on the avoidance of double taxation. In particular, these agreements provide for the following guarantees and safeguards:

- national treatment (each party treats investors of the other party with at least the same level of favour that such party applies to investors of its own state in similar situations, etc.);
- most-favoured-nation treatment (each party treats investors of the other party with at least the same level of favour that such party applies to investors of any third state in similar situations, etc.);
- minimum standards (each party treats investments of investors of the other party according to international law).

2.5.2 Rights of Investors

[134] The following rights of investors are provided for by the legislation of Belarus:

- the right to exercise property rights and intangible rights in accordance with legislation of Belarus;
- recognition of exclusive rights to intellectual property;
- the right to grant land plots for use, lease, title, in accordance with legislation of Belarus on land usage and land protection;
- the right to create a commercial entity within the territory of Belarus with any amount of investment, in any legal form provided for by legislation of Belarus (restrictions: investment is not allowed to be made in the property of legal entities holding a dominant position in the Belarusian goods market without a permit of the antimonopoly body of Belarus, or in activities prohibited by the laws of Belarus);
- the right to make monetary contributions in the authorised fund in foreign currency and/or BYN and non-monetary contributions duly assessed in money terms in accordance with the procedure stipulated by legislation of Belarus;
- the right to privileges and preferences established in accordance with the laws of Belarus and/or international legal acts binding upon Belarus;
- the right to enter into an investment agreement with Belarus;
- the right to engage foreign citizens and stateless persons for labour activities in Belarus.

2.5.3 Special Legal Regimes

[135] The Belarusian legislation endows some territories with special legal status, in particular, FEZ, the HTP and the Great Stone Industrial Park.

[136] Currently, Belarus has six FEZ: FEZ Minsk (www.fezminsk.by), FEZ Brest (www.fez.brest.by), FEZ Gomel-Raton (www.gomelraton.com), FEZ Mogilev (www.fezmogilev.by), FEZ Grodnoinvest (www.grodnoinvest.com), and FEZ Vitebsk (www.fez-vitebsk.com). All Belarusian FEZs are free to operate up until 31 December 2049.

Free Economic Zones

[137] FEZ residents are business entities of Belarus or IEs duly registered by the FEZ Administration in accordance with the procedure defined by the applicable FEZ legislation.

[138] In order to obtain the FEZ resident status, a corporate entity or an IE must comply with all the following requirements:

- such entity/entrepreneur must be located within FEZ territory;
- such entity/entrepreneur must conclude a Business Environment Agreement with FEZ Administration on the terms of activities within FEZ;
- the volume of investments must be at least EUR1 m or at least EUR500 000 where investments are made within three years from the date of the FEZ agreement;
- the creation and/or development of manufacturing capacities aimed at exporting products and/or import substitution.

[139] FEZ residents must carry out their activities under the existing laws and under the FEZ Business Environment Agreement. The FEZ Business Environment Agreement is executed between a business entity/IE and the relevant FEZ Administration. The FEZ Business Environment Agreement is executed for the duration of the project under development. The model form of the FEZ Business Environment Agreement is approved by the relevant FEZ Administration.

[140] Tax regimes in FEZ offer a number of privileges and benefits (exemption from payments of some duties, other payments, and/or reduced tax rates). Tax privileges for FEZ residents do not apply to banks and insurance companies, public catering, gambling activities, electronic interactive games, securities businesses, sale of goods (or works, or services) produced (performed) by using fixed assets owned (or possessed under some other real property right) by a FEZ resident, and/or by using labour of FEZ resident employees, outside the FEZ territory. Privileges under the FEZ regime apply to FEZ residents with regard to their realisation of:

- in-house goods (works, services) produced by residents within the FEZ territory for export under foreign trade agreements concluded with non-residents;
- in-house goods (works, services) produced by residents within the FEZ territory for other FEZ residents;
- in-house goods produced by residents within the FEZ territory to non-residents outside Belarus;
- in-house goods produced by residents within the FEZ territory to non-residents outside Belarus on the basis of commission agreements, instructions or other similar civil contracts concluded by these residents of the FEZ, who are participants in a holding registered in Belarus, with a commission agent (attorney), other similar person who is a participant in the same holding:

No.	Tax Benefit	Tax Benefit Terms and Duration	
1	Exemption from profit tax	Profit of FEZ residents from the sale of in-house goods (works, services) is exempt from profit tax	
2	Exemption from real estate tax	Within three years from the quarter of registration as a FEZ resident, regardless of the direction of use of real estate units*.	For objects located on the territory of the corresponding FEZ, regardless of the direction of their use, subject to the sale in the previous quarter of goods (works, services), which are subject to the peculiarities of taxation of FEZ.

No.	Tax Benefit	Tax Benefit Terms and Duration
		With regard to facilities acquired for title (constructed) in FEZ territory irrespective of their purpose of use.
3	Exemption from land tax	With regard to land plots of FEZ residents located within the boundaries of a FEZ and granted to them after their registration as FEZ residents for construction of facilities. The benefit is valid for no more than five years from the quarter in which the registration as a FEZ resident took place, but does not apply to land plots provided for temporary use or lease and not returned in due time.
		With regard to land plots of FEZ residents located within the boundaries of FEZ, irrespective of the purpose of their use, provided the sale of goods (works, services), which is subject to the peculiarities of taxation of FEZ. The benefit does not apply to land plots provided for temporary use, leased and not returned in a timely manner in accordance with the legislation, unauthorised occupations, as well as land plots where the land tax rate increased by coefficient 3 is applied.
4	Exemption from Value Added Tax (VAT)	With regard to imported goods placed under the customs procedure of the free customs zone (import VAT).
5	Exemption from rental payments for state-owned land plots upon the end of construction	With regard to land plots located within corresponding FEZ territories irrespective of their purpose of use; therewith the mentioned privilege will be applied from the first day of the first month to the last day of the third month of a quarter if, within the immediately preceding quarter, such FEZ resident has realised goods (works, services) of own production

No.	Tax Benefit	Tax Benefit Terms and Duration
		With respect to the land plots of FEZ residents located within the boundaries of the FEZ and provided to them after registration as residents of the FEZ for the construction of facilities. The benefit is granted from the quarter on which the date of registration as residents of the FEZ falls, to the quarter inclusive, in which the last of the construction projects was commissioned. The benefit is valid for no more than five years from the date of registration.

* For reference only: This benefit is not applied to real estate units which have been acquired or transferred by a FEZ resident for rent, lease or other compensated or non-compensated usages.

[141] Any entity importing goods into a FEZ may declare the 'free customs zone' (hereinafter – 'FCZ') customs procedure. Both foreign and Customs Union goods may be placed under the FCZ procedure and used on the FEZ territory. Such FCZ goods are exempt from customs duties, taxes, special anti-dumping and compensation duties. An entity placing goods under the FCZ procedure does not need to secure the payment of customs duties.

[142] Goods must be removed from the FEZ territory according to the following rules:

- foreign FCZ goods without modifications must be removed outside the Customs Union territory without paying customs duties (the 're-export' customs procedure);
- foreign FCZ goods without modifications must be removed to the remaining Customs Union territory (outside FEZ) subject to import customs duties (the 'release for domestic consumption' customs procedure);
- Customs Union FCZ goods without modifications (and goods produced in a FEZ exclusively from Customs Union goods) must be removed outside the Customs Union territory subject to export customs duties and taxes (the 'export' customs procedure);
- Customs Union FCZ goods without modifications (and goods produced in a FEZ exclusively from Customs Union goods) must be removed to the remaining Customs Union territory (outside FEZ) without paying customs duties/ taxes (the 're-import' customs procedure);
- goods produced in a FEZ using foreign goods in compliance with the sufficient processing criteria and exported outside the Customs Union territory are treated as Customs Union goods and are therefore subject to export customs duties and taxes (the 'export' customs procedure);
- goods produced in a FEZ using foreign goods without observing the sufficient processing criteria and exported outside the Customs Union territory

are treated as foreign goods and must be exported without paying customs duties and taxes (the 're-export' customs procedure).

High-Tech Park

[143] The HTP offers the preferential tax regime provided by Belarus specifically for IT companies. The HTP was established in 2005. Its ultimate goal is to increase competitiveness of the national economy by boosting the information and communication sector. Decree No. 8 extended the effective period of the HTP special regime till 1 January 2049.

[144] HTP residency may be acquired by a legal entity or an IE registered in Belarus. Both Belarusian citizens and foreign individuals and companies may act as founders of such legal entities. As of 1 January 2023, according to the HTP website, there are 1 065 residents of the Belarusian HTP – they are engaged in software development and rendering IT services to clients from sixty seven countries all around the globe.

[145] The legislation of Belarus specifies certain requirements for applicants intending to join the HTP:

- an applicant must carry out activities in an innovative/hi-tech sphere permitted by the legislation for the HTP;
- an applicant must have a business plan to implement as an HTP resident.

[146] On 12 April 2023, Decree No. 102 'On the development of the HTP' came into force, according to which the structure and distribution of functions of the HTP were changed, namely: the management company and the secretariat of the HTP Supervisory Board (which the HTP Administration joins) are being created.

[147] The following documents must be submitted to the secretariat of the HTP Supervisory Board in order to join the HTP:

- an application;
- copies of its statutory document and state registration certificate;
- a business plan proposed for implementation as an HTP resident.

[148] The business plan is the key factor for approving registration of an entity as an HTP resident. Such business plan must include information on the applying legal entity, its history and achievements, a development strategy with regard to the HTP, a description of its major products to be manufactured, as well as an analysis of potential markets for selling them. A business plan must contain an estimate of the main economic indicators planned for the period of its implementation, including sales revenues, project profitability, as well as sources and amounts of its funding and areas for reinvestment of future profits, and other required information.

[149] The secretariat of the HTP Supervisory Board will examine the submitted documents and will then furnish them to the HTP Supervisory Board as well as the management company together with its opinion on the advisability or inexpediency of the applicant's registration as an HTP resident. The final decision on registration (or refusal to register) will be made within two months from the date of

application, with the exception of the need for scientific and technical expertise (in this case, the decision-making period will be up to three months).

[150] HTP residents may carry out only the types of business activities specified in the HTP Regulation and declared in their business projects during registration. In order to pursue another (not declared) activity type, a resident must submit a new (supplementary) business project for the approval of the HTP Supervisory Board. Violation of this rule will entail deprivation of HTP resident status and cancellation of all privileges.

[151] At present, HTP residents are entitled to carry out the following types of activities:

- analysis, design and development of software for information systems;
- data processing activities using third parties' or own software;
- fundamental and applied research, experimental development in the field of natural and technical sciences (R&D works connected with HTP activities, including information society development) and implementation of R&D results;
- development or separate stages of development (research, design (construction), testing, technical tests) of materials, technologies, devices and systems of micro-, opto- and nanoelectronics, microelectromechanics and implementation of their results, selling materials, technologies, devices and systems of micro-, opto- and nanoelectronics, microelectromechanics developed by an HTP resident and compatible built-in software;
- development or separate stages of development (research, design (construction), testing, engineering tests) of technologies, devices and systems of mechatronics, built-in systems, software and hardware tools, software and hardware complexes, components and computer equipment and implementation of such development results involving (or not involving) services for their manufacturing application;
- development (research, design (construction), testing, engineering tests) of data transmission equipment, radio location, radio navigation, radio communication, radio control, radio frequency identification technologies/ devices/systems, and implementation of such development results involving (or not involving) services for their manufacturing application;
- development or separate stages of development (research, design (construction), prototyping, testing, engineering tests), manufacture of science-intensive materials, technologies, hi-tech devices/systems, embedded systems, soft hardware facilities, software-hardware appliances and associated software, and implementation of such products and/or development results involving (or not involving) services for their manufacturing application;
- activities in technical and/or cryptographical protection of information including application of Electronic Digital Signatures (EDSs);
- designing, development, implementation (separate implementation stages), support, maintenance and operation of software and/or soft hardware facilities/appliances using cloud-computing technology, i.e., a technology

providing computing resources and software as services to users via telecommunication networks by means of automated processes of computer power allocation and application deployment;

– consulting services for corporate entities in the sphere of commercial activities and management, involving services pertaining to the complex control of development processes and implementation of information systems/technologies;

– analysing informational needs of legal entities and individuals (system analysis, business analysis), consulting in the application of information technologies for the innovation (re-engineering) of business processes involving the development of technical specifications for information systems and software;

– auditing data systems and software in the process of their development, implementation and operation, in terms of their compliance with users' technical requirements and/or informational needs;

– services pertaining to the system support and maintenance of computer facilities and local computer networks of public information systems;

– automated services in searching, selection, processing and sorting data upon third parties' requests, furnishing information to third parties via the Internet network;

– designing, development, implementation and operation of software and/or soft hardware facilities based on or using transaction block registers (block chain technology), other distributed decentralised information systems, in particular using cryptographic data protection facilities;

– designing, maintenance, operation and realisation of unmanned control systems for vehicles;

– designing, maintenance and realisation of finance information technologies, software and hardware technologies for the financial sphere (contact-free cashless settlement technologies, mobile payments, electronic biddings, etc.);

– creation and training of neuron networks and other algorithms in the specialised spheres of artificial intelligence, implementation of results of such activities;

– development or separate stages of development of biotechnology, medical, aviation, space technology, implementation of results of such activities;

– activities pertaining to services rendered to non-residents of Belarus using software (soft hardware) developed by HTP residents involving the management of auxiliary production, administrative and business processes of corporate entities (business process outsourcing);

– services involving the provision of software and technical capacities via the Internet network, enabling contacts and transactions between sellers and buyers (including the provision of a real-time Internet trading site), using software (soft hardware) developed by HTP residents;

– advertising and intermediary services, except for bank transactions, conducted in the Internet network using software developed by HTP residents;

- activities pertaining to the development, implementation and realisation of the Internet-of-Things concept (a network of physical objects fitted with embedded interaction technologies);
- educational activities in information & communication technologies, in particular via the Internet network, according to study programmes approved by the secretariat of the HTP Supervisory Board;
- software publishing which means usage by one person (publisher) of software developed by another person (writer) under a licence agreement or another type of agreement between them, providing for publisher's proprietary rights to such software for the purpose of its commercialisation by the published anywise, in particular by means of modification/adaptation, promotion, or distribution;
- services involving the creation and placement of digital tokens via the Internet network, in particular, services involving the promotion of digital tokens, consulting and other related services;
- crypto-platform operator activities;
- crypto-currency exchange operator activities;
- mining;
- other activities involving digital tokens, in particular, activities which can be characterised as professional/exchange securities activities, investment fund activities, securitisation activities, and operations involving the creation and placement of own digital tokens;
- activities involving the promotion of software, in particular, computer games, for any platforms, including marketing, advertising and/or consulting services rendered via the Internet network;
- services of data processing centres;
- services based on cloud-computing technologies using software and/or soft hardware appliances/complexes developed by HTP residents;
- activities involving the creation of audio/video/music compositions using software developed by HTP residents, creation of graphical/video materials using computer graphics;
- activities in cybersports, in particular training of cyber teams, arrangement and holding of competitions, arrangement of broadcasting of such competitions, arrangement of advertising services pertaining to such activities.

[152] The above list is not exhaustive – the HTP Supervisory Board may grant a company the right to pursue other types of activities under the HTP regime, provided that such activities are directly related to the sphere of new and high technologies.

[153] Furthermore, HTP residents are entitled to:

- lease out immovable property (portions of such property) owned by an HTP resident;
- grant loans to employees out of HTP residents' net profits;
- create Belarusian or foreign corporate entities, acquire, alienate and otherwise dispose of shares (capital stock, equity interests) in the statutory funds of legal entities, including foreign legal entities, receive dividends;

- receive proceeds (income) from software developed with the participation of such HTP resident or distributed by such HTP resident (for instance, from advertisements placed within such software, paid subscription to software, fees for additional functionality, etc.);
- dispose of property (including immovable property) which has been used by such HTP resident for at least twelve months from the date of acquisition;
- provide gratuitous (sponsorship) aid to Belarusian educational institutions under gratuitous aid agreements;
- act as the project owner (developer) with regard to permanent buildings erected for own needs or for its employees' needs;
- engage in activities involving transactions via smart contracts, usage and exchange of electronic money, creation of electronic wallets.

[154] The following tax privileges and other benefits pertaining to mandatory budget payments are provided to HTP residents.

[155] There are exemptions from:

(1) profit tax (except profit tax payable in the capacity of tax agent; profit tax on the disposal of an HTP resident's property; profit tax on certain business activities subject to a diminished (9%) tax rate as defined by legislation);

(2) VAT on sales of goods (works, services, property rights) within the territory of Belarus (this privilege does not apply to lease/alienation of an HTP resident's property, including real estate);

(3) land tax on land plots within the HTP for a period of construction of permanent structures (buildings and constructions) on such land plots by HTP residents in order to carry out their activities, but for no more than three years;

(4) real estate tax on real estate objects of HTP residents located within the HTP territory (except for objects leased out by HTP residents);

(5) offshore duty on settlements for advertising, marketing or intermediary services, and on dividends paid to an HTP resident's founders/participants;

(6) personal income tax on incomes drawn by natural persons from the sale of participatory shares (capital stock) of HTP residents which have been in such natural person's ownership continuously for at least 365 calendar days from the date of acquisition;

(7) 'import' VAT on sales made in Belarus to HTP residents by foreign entities not having a permanent establishment in Belarus, with respect to:
   (a) proprietary rights to intellectual property objects;
   (b) advertising, marketing, consulting services;
   (c) data processing services;
   (d) services involving development, modification, testing and/or technical support/maintenance of software;

(e) hosting services (accommodation of information resources on servers and providing access to such resources), including web hosting (in particular, bundled services for the purpose of accommodating/managing websites);

(f) services involving searching and/or furnishing information on prospective buyers to customers;

(g) services involving creation of and provision of access to databases.

[156] This privilege provides an exemption from VAT on purchases of foreign web hosting and/or advertising services and allows cooperation with online app stores and platforms without extra VAT costs.

[157] Compulsory insurance contributions are not charged on the portion of an HTP resident's employees' income exceeding one average monthly salary in Belarus which is received in the month preceding the month of payment of compulsory insurance contributions. Thus, compulsory insurance contributions will be calculated and paid to the Social Security Fund according to the amount of average salary in Belarus, irrespective of employees' actual salary. Consequently, the amount of compulsory insurance contributions will not depend on HTP residents' salaries, which allows for significant money saving.

[158] As a general rule, the 9% tax rate is applied to income of individuals received within one calendar year from HTP residents under employment contracts, as well as to the income of HTP residents who are IEs, unlike the standard 13% rate of income tax applied to private individuals normally. However, the standard 13% rate is now in effect till 1 January 2025.

[159] A reduced (0%) rate applies to income of foreign entities having no permanent representative office in Belarus, in respect of:

– disposal of participatory shares (equity interests, capital stock) of HTP residents (or portions thereof), provided they have been in such foreign entity's beneficial ownership continuously for at least 365 calendar days;
– activities involving data processing, data allocation, web hosting;
– services involving processing of data and compilation of customised reports;
– services involving input and processing of data (including database management, data storage, database access);
– arrangement of advertisements in the Internet network;
– activities of web portals supporting websites using search engines, for the purpose of creation and maintenance of large Internet address/content databases in formats allowing prompt data search;
– provision of server disk space and/or communication channel for data allocation, and related maintenance services;
– debt obligations of any type, regardless of execution mode;
– royalties;
– intermediary services;
– advertising services.

[160] A reduced 5% income tax rate is applied to foreign companies having no permanent representative office in Belarus in respect of their dividends received from HTP residents.

[161] A reduced 9% income tax rate is applied to:

– incomes from the disposal of participatory shares (or portions thereof), equity interests (or portions thereof) in a business entity;
– incomes from the sale of an enterprise as a property complex;
– incomes from the sale (redemption) of securities;
– interest income on loans;
– dividends from sources outside Belarus;
– participant's (shareholder's) income pertaining to company liquidation, participant's withdrawal/exclusion, in an amount exceeding his/her contribution to the authorised fund or such participant's actual expenses on the acquisition of a participatory/equity share;
– participant's (shareholder's) income in the form of the value of a participatory share (value of equity interest, stocks at par) in the same entity, and/or in the form of increased value of capital stocks due to equity capital increase, where any member's participatory share changes by more than 0.01%;
– a positive difference between the value of lent/borrowed property and the value of property transferred for the purpose of loan redemption.

[162] The residents are exempted from customs duties and VAT on goods imported into Belarus and pertaining to projects implemented by HTP residents. To apply this privilege, an entity needs to obtain a resolution from the secretariat of the HTP Supervisory Board on the intended use of such goods.

[163] In consideration of the privileges granted, all HTP residents must remit 1% of their revenues in each quarter to the secretariat of the HTP Supervisory Board.

[164] In the sphere of currency control, HTP residents are:

– exempt from the forex surrender liability, where such foreign currency is earned within the course of their authorised business activities;
– allowed to use electronic money issued by foreign companies;
– allowed to buy foreign currency in the internal money market without restrictions as to its usage;
– allowed to conduct capital flow currency operations and to open accounts in foreign banks upon notification to the NB (no permission by the NB is required).

[165] In carrying out foreign economic activities, HTP residents:

– do not need to comply with the mandatory terms and procedures pertaining to foreign trade transactions;
– may conclude foreign economic agreements by implicative conduct.

[166] In the sphere of accounting, HTP residents are entitled to:

– autonomously compile source accounting documents reflecting transactions in the accounting books;

- record a set of homogenous commercial transactions within one calendar month by a single accounting document (and specifically by an autonomously compiled document);
- make use of source accounting documents issued by non-residents in a foreign language, in particular in electronic form.

[167] In the sphere of migration procedures:

- HTP residents need not obtain special permits for labour activities in order to engage foreign workers.
- A visa-free entry regime is provided for the owners of HTP residents, foreign employees of HTP residents and employees of property holders, founders and participants of HTP residents provided they are legal entities.

Great Stone Industrial Park

[168] The Great Stone Industrial Park is a transnational project aimed at creating favourable conditions for investment and trade cooperation. The Park's advantageous location and privileged business regime provide investors with favourable access to the CIS and European Union (EU) markets.

[169] The Industrial Park is a platform for projects developing the following spheres of activity:

- electronics;
- telecommunications;
- pharmaceuticals;
- fine chemistry;
- biotechnologies;
- machine building;
- new materials;
- integrated logistics;
- electronic commerce;
- activities in storing and processing large volumes of data;
- social and cultural activities;
- research and advanced development.

[170] The Industrial Park is notable among other economic zones for the following preferences.

[171] The business regime offered by the Industrial Park features an unprecedented selection of tax and customs preferences:

- Exemption from the profit tax – within ten years from the date of first profit accrual, thereafter at half standard rate (standard rate is 18%).
- Dividend tax rate is 0% for five years from the date of the first dividend distribution plus exemption from the offshore duty (i.e., dividends may be received free of taxes in Belarus).
- A reduced 5% royalty tax till 2027.
- Exemption from real estate tax.

– Exemption from land tax.
– A reduced 9% personal income tax rate for Industrial Park employees (instead of the standard 13% rate), plus Social Security Fund contributions may be paid in accordance with the national average wage (instead of the standard rate which is five times bigger). For instance, if an employee has a monthly take-home pay equivalent to USD1 500, the Belarusian employer has to pay USD820 of tax and non-tax payments to various funds, while a resident of the Industrial Park will normally have to pay only USD286 (three times less).
– Social Security Fund contributions need not be paid for foreign employees.
– Industrial Park residents may apply the 'FEZ' procedure (i.e., they may import goods to be later exported (including goods processed) outside the EAEU territory without paying VAT and customs duties).
– Goods produced by the Industrial Park residents within the 'FCZ' are exempt from 'import VAT', provided they are realised in Belarus.
– Revenues pertaining to most operations and services performed for Industrial Park residents by foreign companies are exempt from VAT. Such operations/services include auditing, consulting, marketing, legal, engineering, advertising and other services.

[172] The Industrial Park is the main investment project of Belarus in the real economy sector. Its fundamental legal principles and guarantees are stipulated by the Agreement between the Government of Belarus and the Government of the People's Republic of China on the China-Belarus Industrial Park. However, the Industrial Park is open for investors from all over the globe and imposes no obligations on residents to use Belarusian or Chinese goods, services, etc.:

– cooperation with residents and investors is arranged on the basis of a 'one stop service' principle;
– the Industrial Park residents are granted the most favourable business regime in Belarus as compared to other modes of treatment (where any more advantageous business regimes are established elsewhere, they will immediately apply to the Industrial Park residents as well);
– all guarantees and assurances stipulated by the Belarusian legislation apply to the Industrial Park residents, in particular, international treaties and the grandfather clause guaranteeing that no changes in legislation (with minor exceptions) will impact the Industrial Park residents (in terms of taxation – at least till 2027);
– any inspections of Park residents may be performed only in exceptional cases and only as agreed by the Administration.

[173] Obtaining Industrial Park resident status is a standalone administrative procedure requiring compliance with two conditions.

[174] *Location*: only legal entities founded in Belarus and located within the territory of the Industrial Park can be registered as Industrial Park residents. Thus, in order to be registered as an Industrial Park resident, a company must be located

within the Industrial Park territory. If a company is founded directly within the Industrial Park territory it does not need to change its legal address to become a resident of the Industrial Park. The procedure for the creation and registration of a legal entity in the Industrial Park territory is described below. An existing legal entity registered by another registering body (not by the Industrial Park Administration) may also become an Industrial Park resident. However, before applying for the Industrial Park residency, such legal entity must notify the Industrial Park Administration of its relocation.

[175] *Investment project implementation:* the second requirement for the Industrial Park residency is implementing an investment project in a prescribed sphere on the Industrial Park territory.

[176] Any entity applying for residency in the Industrial Park must prepare the following documents.

[177] *Application:* an application must be prepared according to the model form prescribed by the Head of the Industrial Park Administration, and must specify, in particular, information on the investment project, type (types) of business activity planned to be conducted in the Industrial Park, the volumes and terms of investments. The application form is available on the Industrial Park website on the Internet.

[178] Originals and copies of the state registration certificate and the constituent documents verified by the company CEO or duly authorised official. Company Charter (Articles of Association) is the 'constituent document' for this purpose.

[179] *Investment project rationale:* investment project rationale is the document containing the main aspects of the prospective investment project. It must be compiled according to the model form prescribed by the Head of the Industrial Park Administration. An investment project rationale must be approved by the company CEO or another duly authorised official. Investment project rationale should include:

- a description of the project and the products;
- an analysis of market outlets, marketing strategy;
- concrete methods to create and develop high-quality production facilities competitive in external markets;
- a production plan;
- an investment plan;
- a project performance evaluation;
- a project schedule chart.

[180] *Draft agreement on Park operational conditions:* this draft must be compiled according to the model form prescribed by the Head of the Industrial Park Administration. The draft agreement must be signed by the company CEO or another duly authorised official.

[181] Procedure for gaining Park resident status:

Financial Criterion	*Business Line Criterion**
– Stated amount of investment – at least USD500 000 (where the term of investment is at most three years) / at least USD5 m (where the term of investment is more than three years)	– Electronics, telecommunications, pharmaceuticals, fine chemistry, biotechnologies, machine building, new materials, complex logistics, e-commerce, data storage/processing, social/cultural activities.
– For R&D projects – at least USD500 000	– R&D projects

* If a legal entity desires to carry out another type of activity or to define other investment volumes, it must submit such proposal to the Industrial Park Administration.

[182] The Industrial Park Administration is authorised to make decisions on the registration of a legal entity as an Industrial Park resident. The Industrial Park Administration will examine the submitted documents and approve (or refuse) the registration of an applicant within five business days. An applicant will be refused the Industrial Park residency status in the following cases:

- the application and/or attached documents have been prepared in violation of the mandatory requirements;
- the applicant has failed to submit any of the required documents;
- applicant's location fails to comply with the Industrial Park location requirement;
- applicant's prospective business activity and/or volumes of investment do not comply with the Industrial Park's main areas of activity and/or prescribed volumes of investment, unless the Industrial Park Administration decides otherwise;
- applicant's prospective business activity does not comply with the Industrial Park's main business objectives;
- the Industrial Park territory does not have an available land plot suitable for the characteristics of the proposed investment project as stated in the application;
- the proposed investment project involves any business activity prohibited in the Industrial Park.

[183] The date of the Industrial Park Administration's decision to admit the applicant is the date of registration of such applicant as an Industrial Park resident.

'Bremino–Orsha' Special Economic Zone (SEZ)

[184] 'Bremino-Orsha' SEZ project is aimed at improving the Belarusian logistical system in order to optimise the flows of cargos/goods from manufacturers to consumers in the EU and the EAEU. 'Bremino-Orsha' SEZ is designed to accommodate projects in the following spheres:

- wholesale trade;
- manufacturing industry;
- electronic commerce;
- research and development activities;
- activities involving logistical services, postal services;
- activities involving information, office, administrative, ancillary services;
- activities involving railroad, motor car, air transportation, other ancillary activities involving shipping operations.

[185] 'Bremino-Orsha' SEZ's regime offers the following preferences:

- exemption from profit tax with respect to residents' profits from sales of in-house goods/works/services produced within the SEZ for nine years;
- exemption from real estate tax for twenty years;
- exemption from dividend profit tax (and similar taxes) for five years, starting from the first calendar year of dividend distribution;
- a lower royalty tax rate (5%) till 1 January 2028;
- exemption from offshore duty;
- exemption from exchange rate differences from non-operating gains/losses for the purpose of profit tax till 1 January 2033;
- full deduction of VAT in construction/fitting projects, exemption from VAT with respect to sales and leasing of real estate units to residents till 1 January 2033;
- legal regime guaranteed till 1 January 2028;
- the FCZ procedure may be applied (i.e., goods may be imported without paying VAT and customs duties, provided such goods (including processed goods) will be further exported beyond the territory of the EAEU).

[186] Obtaining residency in 'Bremino-Orsha' SEZ is a standalone procedure. Applicants must meet the following conditions.

[187] A legal entity created on the territory of Belarus and located in 'Bremino-Orsha' SEZ may be registered as a resident of 'Bremino-Orsha' SEZ. Such a company may be created immediately in 'Bremino-Orsha' SEZ – in such a case no change of domicile (location address) is required for residency status. Also, an existing company registered by another body (i.e., not by 'Bremino-Orsha' SEZ's managing company) may acquire residency in 'Bremino-Orsha' SEZ. However, prior to applying for residency, such company must notify 'Bremino-Orsha' SEZ's managing company of the change of location.

[188] An applicant must implement (or schedule) an investment project in a certain prescribed sphere within the SEZ, with an investment volume of at least USD500 000 (where such project will be accomplished within three years or involves any R&D activities), or USD 5 m (where such project will be accomplished within five years). Where an applicant (legal entity) wishes to be engaged in another type of activity or offer another investment volume, it must submit such proposal to 'Bremino-Orsha' SEZ's managing company.

[189] In order to obtain residency in 'Bremino-Orsha' SEZ, an applicant must submit the following documents.

[190] *Application:* the application must be completed according to the form approved by the director of 'Bremino-Orsha' SEZ's managing company and must indicate, particularly, the investment project, the sphere and the type(s) of business activities proposed by the applicant, volumes and timeframes of investments. An application form is available at 'Bremino-Orsha' SEZ's website (Bremino-sez.by).

[191] Copies of state registration certificates and constituent documents duly attested by CEO (acting CEO). 'Constituent documents' mean a company's articles of association.

[192] *Investment project duly approved by CEO (acting CEO):* investment project is a document specifying the main aspects of the proposed activity. It must be compiled in accordance with the form approved by the director of 'Bremino-Orsha' SEZ's managing company. An investment project form is available at 'Bremino-Orsha' SEZ's website (Bremino-sez.by). An investment project must specify the following:

- The project's main point, characteristics of the applicant (legal entity), a description of its products.
- An analysis of sales areas, validation of marketing strategy.
- A production schedule.
- An investment schedule.
- A project feasibility research.
- A project progress chart.

[193] Draft agreement on 'Bremino-Orsha' SEZ's operational environment, specifying terms and conditions duly agreed upon with 'Bremino-Orsha' SEZ's managing company and signed by the applicant's CEO or another duly authorised official.

[194] Decisions on granting residency status in 'Bremino-Orsha' SEZ are rendered by 'Bremino-Orsha' SEZ's managing company. Decisions to register a company or to refuse residency are made within three business days at most. The date of 'Bremino-Orsha' SEZ's managing company's decision to admit the applicant is the date of registration of such applicant as a resident of 'Bremino-Orsha' SEZ.

Business Activities in Orsha District, Vitebsk Region

[195] The following preferences will be applied till 31 December 2023 (with minor exceptions):

- a lower tax rate under the Simplified Taxation System (6% for other Belarusian regions, while in Orsha district only 1% with respect to proceeds from sales of goods of own making, and 2% with respect to proceeds from sales of works/services of own making);
- lower Social Security Fund contributions for employers (retirement insurance constitutes 24% instead of 28%);

– exemption from fees normally paid for special permits for foreigners' labour activity;
– no interest is charged in cases of tax deferral or tax payment by instalments;
– VAT sums paid under construction projects may be accepted for deduction without incurring output VAT;
– EU, EAEU, Chinese construction regulations/rules may be applied in design projects, without adapting them to Belarusian norms;
– exemption from VAT, instead of tax payment by instalments, will be used for foreign process equipment and spare parts imported under 0% import duty.

2.5.4 Guarantees of the Investors

[196] The Investments Law guarantees to investors:

(1) protection from uncompensated nationalisation and requisition;
(2) unrestricted transfer outside the territory of Belarus of compensation received as a result of nationalisation; however, such nationalisation is possible only in cases of natural disasters, accidents, epidemics, epizootic diseases and other cases of emergency for the benefit of society at the discretion of state bodies;
(3) the right of an investor whose property was placed in requisition to judicially claim the return of such property, if the circumstances of such requisition are no longer valid;
(4) unconditional transfer (*see* paragraph [193]) outside the territory of Belarus of incomes (profits) and other legally obtained monetary funds connected with investments within the territory of Belarus as well as payments made in favour of a foreign investor and connected with investments, including:
  (a) monetary funds received by foreign investors after partial or full termination of investment activities in the territory of Belarus, including monetary funds received by foreign investors due to disposal of investments or property created as a result of investments, or other objects of civil rights;
  (b) monetary funds constituting outstanding wages to foreign citizens and stateless persons performing labour activities under labour contracts;
  (c) monetary funds due to foreign investors under a judicial decision.
(5) protection from unfavourable changes to tax legislation (this guarantee applies to investors who have entered into an investment agreement with Belarus).

[197] *See* paragraph [196] point (4) after payment of taxes, duties and other mandatory payments established by legislation of Belarus.

[198] The local Belarusian financing market remains underdeveloped, resulting in a lack of variety of financing options. Generally, local and foreign investors may freely use their own internal funds or borrowed assets. Foreign entities acquiring

Belarusian companies are typically self-financed, meaning they obtain financing (if any) by using their established sources of financing in other countries.

[199] It is rare for the Belarusian banking market to finance large-scale investments, including M&A projects. Therefore, obtaining sufficient financing from local banks will probably involve high interest rates whether for local or for foreign investors. For local banks, it is unusual to finance cost-demanding M&A deals, and the terms of financing, including interest rates, will vary from bank to bank.

[200] As domestic debt financing is generally unaffordable and hard to obtain, foreign and local investors may seek foreign bank loans. The International Finance Corporation (IFC) and the EAEU Development Bank (EDB) have all been active in Belarus and offer a potential source of financing for investors in Belarus.

[201] Leveraged and mezzanine financing remains quite novel in Belarus and potentially may be, but is not in practice yet used, for M&A deals. For a local investor, it is also possible to issue bonds on the local capital market and to apply the attracted funds towards M&A deal financing (however, it is a rare case in practice, as the Belarusian capital market lacks liquidity).

[202] It is permissible for a foreign lender to take security over local immovable property, except for cases where the security object is land or a leasehold right of land. Establishing collateral over the land or the right of land leasehold is limited in Belarus and is permitted only for certain leaseholders providing financing to local investors. Namely, these leaseholders are local banks, IFC, EDB, as well as the Export-Import Bank of China and the China Development Bank (concerning land and leasehold rights of land in the Great Stone Industrial Park).

[203] Currency controls over the transfer of funds to foreign lenders for payment of interest or repayment of capital are imposed on local investors only and require them to register these transfers with the local bank. To date, there are no currency restrictions applying to foreign investors acquiring a share in a capital of a Belarusian company or a foreign lender providing financing to foreign investors.

[204] It is permissible for local/domestic companies to hold offshore bank accounts. As of 9 July 2021, the new currency control legislation entered into force removing the necessity to obtain the NB permit for opening an offshore bank account by local companies. The new legislation requires currency agreements concluded by residents of Belarus with non-residents to be registered on a special portal (however, not all agreements with non-residents are subject to registration but those meeting certain criteria).

[205] As regards other currency legislation provisions, generally, the foreign currency regulations in Belarus are not overly restrictive for non-residents. Foreign investors are entitled to conduct currency operations (including exchange operations) and to use foreign currency in Belarus, for example, in M&A deals without any limitations and restrictions.

2.6 Specific Issues of Company/Securities Law

2.6.1 Shareholder Approval

[206] When selling shares to third parties, the participants of an LLC or of an ALC, as well as the company itself, have a preemptive right to purchase the relevant shares. The participant intending to sell the share must send to (a) the other participants and (b) the company itself a notice of its intention to sell the share. The notice must specify the terms of the intended sale. After receiving the notification from the participant, the rest of the participants must send their consent or refusals to purchase the share. If no consent or refusal is received, then the participants are considered to have refused the purchase. If the participants do not exercise their preemptive right to purchase the share, the company itself may exercise the right to acquire it. The will of the company to acquire or refuse to acquire the share is expressed in the form of an appropriate decision by the general meeting of participants. Previously, the preemptive right was also envisaged for CJSCs. However, from 28 April 2021, these peremptory norms have been cancelled. Despite this, the charter of a CJSC may provide for the preemptive right of its shareholders and for the right of the company itself to acquire shares sold by other shareholders. Additional requirements and specifics of selling shares can be stipulated by the charter of the company (e.g., the participant can be obliged to get the consent of other participants to sell shares to one of the participants of the company). At the same time, affiliates (including shareholders owing at least 20% of shares), inspectors (members of inspection commission) of the company, auditors and other persons who have access to close information on the securities market can not sell shares of OJSC or CJSC within six months after acquisition, except for selling to the OJSC or CJSC itself.

[207] If the share was acquired during marriage, then together with the notice of the sale of the share, the participant must send the consent of the spouse to the sale of the share. In the absence of a spouse who can claim a part of the share, the participant informs the other participants and the company about this. It is advisable to place this information at the end of the text of the notification of the sale of the share. If a marriage contract is concluded between the spouses, then the marriage contract is submitted instead of the consent, if in accordance with the contract the consent to the sale of the share is not required.

[208] A different process is established for UEs. There are two ways to sell a UE:

> *Option 1:* Sale of a UE as a property complex. Firstly, it is necessary to register a UE as a property complex (which is considered a real estate) in the research and production state UE 'National Cadastral Agency'. After that, it is necessary to register the transaction (sale and purchase agreement) there. The agreement is considered concluded from the moment of such registration.

Option 2: Sale of a UE through reorganisation (transformation) into another business entity. In accordance with this method, a UE must be initially reorganised into another business entity (e.g., an LLC). After that, it is possible to dispose of its shares.

2.6.2 Executive Authority's Duties

[209] The executive body performs day-to-day management of a company. It may be either a sole executive body (either an individual, usually holding the title of general director, director or a management company) or a managerial board with a chairperson heading this collective executive body. Moreover, a company may transfer the duties of its executive body to the management company.

[210] The executive body is elected by the general meeting of participants of a company or by the board of directors (supervisory board) in accordance with the charter. It also may be elected from among non-participants of the company (Article 54 of the Law on Companies).

[211] The rights and duties of the executive body are determined by law, labour legislation, the company's charter, employment agreement (contract) and/or civil law contracts concluded between the company and the person holding the position. The qualifying, professional and other requirements for the executive body and the procedure for making decisions by that body may also be specified by the appropriate local legal act of the company (Article 54 of the Law on Companies).

[212] The competence of an executive body of the company includes routine management of the activity of the company. It is accountable to the general meeting of participants and to the board of directors (supervisory board), if the formation thereof is provided by law or the charter, and must organise fulfilment of the decisions of those bodies (Article 53 of the Law on Companies).

[213] There are no specific executive body's duties owed to the company, its shareholders/participants or third parties when the company is engaged in an M&A transaction.

[214] Members of the executive bodies of a company, when exercising their rights and fulfilling their duties, must act transparently and in the best interests of the company, honestly and reasonably (Article 33 of the Law on Companies).

[215] Depending on the situation, an executive body may be charged with the following duties: (1) notifying the company's creditors of an impending reorganisation; (2) preparing notices of sale of an entity interest in the statutory fund; (3) deciding to convene an extraordinary general meeting of participants to decide on the issue of acquiring/refusing to acquire an entity interest; (4) ensuring state registration of changes to the company's charter, etc.

2.6.3 Contributions to the Charter Capital

[216] The company's statutory fund determines the minimum amount of property of that company guaranteeing the interests of the creditors thereof (Article 28 of the Law on Companies). As a general rule, the minimum amount of statutory fund is not stipulated by the legislation. But there are exceptions for OJSC, CJSC, banks etc. As a general rule, the statutory fund can be formed within twelve months after the registration of business entity.

[217] The contributions to a company's statutory fund can be things, including monetary funds and securities, and other property, including property rights or other alienable rights, the value of which can be calculated (Article 29 of the Law on Companies).

[218] The statutory fund of LLC, ALC, OJSC, CJSC may not be entirely formed with non-monetary contributions in the form of property rights. In this respect, the amount of property rights may not exceed 50% of the statutory fund. This property right must belong to the founders (participants) based on the right of ownership, right of economic management or operative administration. The property cannot be contributed to a company's statutory fund if the right of disposal thereof is restricted by the owner, by the legislation or by agreement. When any non-monetary contribution (including contributions in the form of property rights) is made to the statutory fund, an official assessment of its value must be performed. In performing an official assessment by shareholders, the assessment report must be examined by an independent expert. However, if the assessment is made by an independent expert, no examination is required (Article 29 of the Law on Companies).

2.6.4 Security Interests

[219] Where the acquisition is being financed by bank loans, the banks may obtain security either from the borrower itself or from any third-party security (e.g., from members of the target group).

General Information

[220] Kinds of security in Belarus may include:

- Mortgages over real property.
- Pledges over movable assets.
- Pledges over shares (for joint-stock companies).
- Participatory interest pledges (for limited liability companies).
- Direct suretyships (corporates/individuals).
- Guarantees (corporates/banks/financial institutions).

[221] Pledge is one of the most common measures for securing fulfilment of obligations in Belarus. When the pledgor does not perform or improperly performs obligations secured by pledge (in a pledge agreement it is usually called an 'event of default'), then the pledged property is seized and sold, while the pledgee's requirements are satisfied from its sale proceeds.

[222] Almost any type of property, with minor exclusions (e.g., property withdrawn from civil circulation), is pledgeable, including things and property rights. Depending on the type of property, basically, two types of pledges are distinguished – pledges of immovable (mortgage) or movable property.

[223] There are some special aspects for pledges over shares:

- the pledged shares cannot be transferred to the possession of the pledgee for the period of the pledge. That is, the pledgor (the owner of the shares which give him the right to participate in the management of the company) continues to participate in the management of the company, despite the fact that the shares are pledged;
- the transfer of securities (including pledge of shares) is carried out with the obligatory registration of the pledge agreement by a broker or depositary.

[224] Pledged property in full secures the pledgee's claims existing on the date of pledge enforcement, including those in respect of interest on the loan amount, penalties, compensation for losses caused by non-performance or improper performance, reimbursement of the pledgee's expenses for maintenance and levying execution on the pledged property, unless otherwise provided by contract.

[225] A pledge arises on the basis of an agreement made in written form.

[226] In a pledge/mortgage agreement, the parties must spell out the object of the agreement, the subject of the pledge/mortgage and its cost, the nature and term of the secured obligations, and the rights and obligations of a party holding a pledged property. In cases where immovable property is pledged, the parties must also indicate the right on the basis of which the subject of the pledge belongs to the pledgor and the regional department of the Agency for state registration of immovable property which has registered this right. Without these conditions, a pledge/mortgage agreement is considered non-concluded, which means that rights and obligations of the parties do not arise.

State Registration

[227] In cases where immovable property is pledged, then a mortgage agreement and the mortgage itself as a kind of restriction are subject to state registration by the Agency for state registration of immovable property, rights and transactions thereon. A mortgage agreement is considered concluded from the moment of its state registration.

[228] In cases where movable property is pledged, information thereon is included in the Register of movable property encumbered by the pledge – this being an informational system on the pledgees' rights to the pledgors' movable property.

Sequence of Satisfying Requirements of Pledgees

[229] As a general rule, pledged property (whether movable or immovable) can be subsequently pledged. A subsequent pledge is allowed if it is not prohibited by the original pledge agreement. In this case, the pledgor is obliged to inform the pledgee about all existing pledges of this property. In the case of a mortgage agreement, if the pledgor has not fulfilled this obligation, the pledgee is entitled to require performance under the main contract.

[230] The appropriate sequence for satisfying the requirements of pledgees depends on whether the pledged property is movable or immovable.

[231] Immovable property: claims of a subsequent mortgagee are satisfied from the pledged property's sale proceeds only after the requirements of the original mortgagee have been satisfied. In other words, priority is given to mortgagees who registered a mortgage agreement with respect to the same immovable property earlier than the other mortgagees.

[232] Movable property: a priority is given to the pledgee posting in an appropriate manner correct information on the pledge in the Register of movable property encumbered with the pledge, regardless of the time of execution of pledge agreements. It should be noted that including information in the Register does not affect entry into force or validity of the pledge agreement.

Foreclosure Procedure on Pledged Property / Pledge Enforcement

[233] When the pledgor does not perform or improperly performs obligations secured by the pledge, the pledgee is entitled to require satisfaction from the proceeds of the pledged property. The fact of non-performance or improper performance is usually called 'an event of default'.

[234] The pledgee's requirements are satisfiable on the ground of:

- a court decision;
- a notarised agreement on levying execution without recourse to legal proceedings.

Enforcement by a Court Decision

[235] Recourse to the court is a general measure of levying execution on the pledged property. In some cases, levying execution on the pledged property can be applied only on the basis of a court decision (e.g., the pledgor is absent and it is impossible to establish his location; the subject of the pledge is property that is limited in circulation).

[236] Realisation of the pledged property is performed in a way defined by the court's decision according to the Belarusian legislation on enforcement proceedings, *inter alia*, by a judicial executor via tender. Bidding price of the realised property (the price which starts the tender) is set by a judicial executor and is based on the property cost provided for in the court decision.

Enforcement by a Foreclosure Agreement

[237] Appeals to the court are avoided, if there is a corresponding notarised foreclosure agreement between the pledgee and the pledgor. Such an agreement is concluded either before or after an event of default. It is recommended to conclude

a foreclosure agreement simultaneously with the pledge agreement. It should provide for the right of the pledgee/pledger/other person (as a matter of choice of the parties) to sell the pledged property on behalf of the pledgor in order to satisfy the pledgee's requirements.

[238] Pledged property is sold via public tender by the pledgee/pledgor/other person specified in the foreclosure agreement. In cases where the pledged property is a private land plot/the right to lease a land plot/capital structures with the simultaneous pledge of a private land plot (lease rights of the land plot) on which these capital structures are located, then the property is to be sold only by the pledgee. The bidding price of the realised property is determined in the foreclosure agreement.

[239] In cases where the amount gained from realisation of property by tender is insufficient, the pledgee is entitled to satisfy his requirements from the cost of other property of the pledgor.

[240] In circumstances where a tender is recognised to be void, the pledgee is entitled to buy the pledged property and to set off the pledgor's indebtedness against it. If the pledgor refuses to buy the pledged property during a period of one month from the tender being announced void, then the pledge ceases to exist.

[241] Notwithstanding the conclusion of a foreclosure agreement, the pledgee maintains the right to apply to the court to levy execution on the pledged property.

[242] Specifics of the pledge of shares are stipulated by the Law on Companies and a Charter of a business entity (e.g., pledgee is entitled to keep shares for itself instead of selling them to third parties).

Insolvency Procedure

[243] In the event of insolvency of the pledger, the pledgee (the creditor) has to send the creditor's requirements to the anti-crisis manager within two months from the date of publication of the information about the beginning of the insolvency proceedings in the journal 'Judicial Bulletin Plus: Economic Justice'. If there is a pledge, the bank's requirements are to be satisfied in the fourth stage after employees' and tax authorities' requirements, if there is no pledge – in the fifth stage.

[244] After the start of the insolvency procedure, the anti-crisis manager has the right to unwind or set aside transactions made by the debtor six months, one year or three years before the start of the insolvency procedure (a suspect period). The grounds for disputing the transaction are:

- the preferred satisfaction of the property requirements of creditor 1 over creditor 2, if the requirements of creditor 2 arose before the conclusion of the transaction with creditor 1;
- if the pledger intentionally caused damage to creditors and party to the contract was aware;
- however, such transactions are difficult to contest in the courts if parties to the contract are not affiliates.

2.6.5 Completion Formalities

For Limited Liability and Additional Liability Companies

[245] After the share purchase agreement is concluded, the buyer must send a written notification to the limited liability company or ALC about the disposal of the share(s) with a copy of the share purchase agreement attached to it. The buyer exercises the rights and bears the obligations of the participant from the moment the company is notified.

[246] The change in the composition of the LLC and ALC is the basis for making appropriate changes and additions to the charter. For the convenience of further usage, the charter can be adopted in a new edition. Changing the charter is within the exclusive competence of the general meeting of the participants. Accordingly, the general meeting approves the new list of participants and makes a decision on amendments and additions to the charter. Changes and amendments to the charter of limited liability or additional liability companies or the charter in a new edition in connection with the change in the composition of the participants are registered at the state authorities (executive committee) within no more than two months.

For CJSCs

[247] Joint-stock companies are not obliged to make changes and amendments to the charter and register them in connection with the change in the composition of the participants. Therefore, a different procedure will be applied to them. After the conclusion of the share purchase agreement, it is necessary to register the agreement with the depositary, then transfer the shares to the buyer's 'depot' account. If the buyer does not have a 'depot' account, then it is necessary to first open such an account. After such transfer is made, the right to the share passes to the buyer.

[248] The buyer of a large block of shares in a CJSC (5 or more % of ordinary shares) is obliged to disclose information about such acquisition within five working days after fixing the ownership of these shares, that is, from the moment the shares are credited to its 'depot' account. Disclosure of information is carried out by sending a message from the buyer to the CJSC, as well as to the Securities Department of the Ministry of Finance. The notification of the acquisition of shares does not influence the validity or invalidity of the transaction. However, the buyer may be held administratively liable in the form of a fine of up to twenty basic units.

2.6.6 Dividends

[249] Participants of an LLC receive income in the form of net profits distributed by the company, and shareholders of a joint-stock company receive income in the form of dividends distributed by the company. Both are paid out from the company's net profits, i.e., the company's profits calculated after deduction of taxes, other obligatory payments, covering the losses of the current periods, etc.

[250] Decisions on distribution of net profits of an LLC and dividends of a joint-stock company are made by the general meeting of participants/shareholders. Net profits in the former are distributed among the participants on a pro-rata basis depending on the value of their participatory interest unless otherwise determined in the charter or by the relevant decision of participants passed unanimously. In the latter case, dividends are declared as a certain amount payable per share.

[251] Joint-stock companies cannot decide on dividend distributions in the following cases: (1) before the statutory fund has been paid in full; (2) the value of the company's net assets is less than its statutory fund and reserve fund, or would be less than such amounts as a result of the payment of a dividend; (3) if the company meets the insolvency thresholds or becomes insolvent as a result of payment of dividends; (4) before the completion of buyout of shares of the company upon the request of its shareholders (Article 72 of the Law on Companies).

[252] LLCs cannot decide on profit distribution in the following circumstances: (1) before the statutory fund has been paid in full; (2) before the company pays out the value of participation interests (part of participation interests) when required by the Law on Companies; (3) if the company meets the insolvency thresholds or becomes insolvent as a result of payment of the profit; (4) the moment the relevant decision is adopted on payment of the profit, the value of the company's net assets is less than its statutory fund and reserve fund, or would be less than such amount as a result of such decision (Article 96 of the Law on Companies).

2.6.7 Purchase of Its Own Shares by a Joint-Stock Company

[253] The general meeting of shareholders takes the decision on purchase by the joint-stock company of its own shares for the following purposes: (1) subsequent sale or gratuitous transfer to the state; (2) subsequent proportional distribution among shareholders; (3) subsequent sale to the investor on conditions provided by the business plan of the company; (4) cancellation of shares; (5) transfer to a foreign or international legal entity, an organisation that is not a legal entity issuing foreign depositary receipts, the sale of shares using foreign depositary receipts; (6) gratuitous transfer or sale to members of the board of directors (supervisory board), the executive body and (or) the employees of this company; or other instances provided for by the legislative acts (Article 77 of the Law on Companies).

[254] A joint-stock company does not have the right to purchase its own shares under the following circumstances: (1) before the statutory fund has been paid in full; (2) if the company meets the insolvency thresholds or becomes insolvent as a result of the purchase of shares; (3) if on the date of the purchase of shares, the cost of net assets of the company is or would be, as a result of the purchase of shares, less than the amount of the joint-stock company and surplus funds; (4) if the nominal value of all shares disposed of by the company exceeds 10% of the statutory fund of the company, except for the case of reduction of the statutory fund; (5) if the shareholder who presented a proposal on the sale of shares of that company is its sole shareholder; (6) before completion of a mandatory buyout of shares of the company upon the request of shareholders in cases provided for by law (Article 77 of the Law on Companies).

Mandatory BuyOut of Shares of a Joint-Stock Company upon the Request of Its Shareholders

[255] The mandatory buyout of shares of a joint-stock company upon the request of shareholders of that company is carried out in the following cases: (1) reorganisation; (2) entering into a major transaction; (3) change of type of the company; (4) making changes and/or additions to the charter concerning the rights of shareholders which entail limitation of those rights. However, only shareholders voting against the aforementioned decisions or shareholders not appropriately notified about the holding of the general meeting of shareholders at which the decisions were adopted are entitled to request a buyout of the shares (Article 78 of the Law on Companies).

[256] Shareholders of a joint-stock company created in the process of privatisation of state property or by means of transformation of lease-holding enterprises, collective (people's) state enterprises, collective farms (agricultural PCs) and state UEs, more than 50% of whose shares belong to the state are not entitled to request the buyout of their own shares in the event of reorganisation thereof in the form of affiliation to that of one or several legal persons, as well as the shareholder who is the sole participant of that joint-stock company (Article 78 of the Law on Companies).

Disclosure of Information by Shareholders of a Joint-Stock Company and by Other Persons Carrying Out Transactions in Its Shares

[257] Before purchase (except for an acquisition of shares in the process of their issuance) of ordinary shares of an OJSC, persons intending to acquire more than 50% of the ordinary shares of an OJSC or a package of shares the acquisition of which would result (except for acquisition of shares in the process of their issuance) in control of more than 50% of the ordinary shares of an OJSC are obliged to disclose information, including their personal data, and information on their intention to carry out such acquisition (Article 58 of the Securities Market Act).

[258] Disclosure of information must be carried out: (1) through the placement of the text of the proposal on the purchase or buying out of the shares at the unified informational resource of the securities market; (2) through publishing (announcing) the text of the proposal to purchase or buyout the shares and sending the text of the published (announced) proposal to the issuer of such shares, to the Securities Department of the Ministry of Finance and to the Stock Exchange Market (Article 58 of the Securities Market Act).

[259] Also, members of the board of directors (supervisory board), members of the management board, and the person exercising the powers of the sole executive body of an OJSC are obliged to inform the board of directors (supervisory board)

about all their transactions in securities of the company, as well as about transactions in securities of that company made by their close relatives (Article 84 of the Law on Companies).

[260] Any person who has become the holder of 5% or more of the ordinary shares of the company must, within five days after registering his right of ownership to those shares, disclose information, including his personal data, and information about such acquisition, as well as about any change as a result of which his stake of ordinary shares of an issuer exceeds 5%, 10%, 15%, 20%, 25%, 30%, 50% or 75%, as the case may be. Disclosure of the information must be carried out by directing a notification to the issuer of the relevant shares, to the Securities Department of the Ministry of Finance, and to the Stock Exchange Market. The procedure for sending a notification and the requirements for its content are established by the Securities Department of the Ministry of Finance (Article 58 of the Securities Market Act).

Priority Right to Purchase the Participatory Interest in an LLC: Purchase of Its Own Participatory Interest by an LLC

[261] Participants of an LLC have the right to sell or otherwise alienate their participatory interest (or part of a participatory interest) (Article 97 of the Law on Companies). Before offering to sell a participatory interest (part of a participatory interest) in the statutory fund of an LLC to a third party, a participant must first offer it to other participants of the company, and in case of their refusal – to the company itself.

[262] Participants of an LLC have a preemptive right to purchase the participatory interest (or part of a participatory interest) in the statutory fund of the company, in proportion to the sizes of their interests in the statutory fund of the company, unless the charter or the decision of the general meeting of participants of the company approved unanimously provides another procedure for exercising the pre-emption right or unless otherwise established by the President of Belarus (Article 98 of the Law on Companies).

[263] In case the participants of an LLC do not exercise their priority right to purchase the participatory interest (or part of the participatory interest) of the participant in the statutory fund of the company within the time limit provided by the charter of the company, the participatory interest (or part of the participatory interest) in the charter capital of the company may be disposed of to the company itself (Article 99 of the Law on Companies).

[264] An LLC within one year after the date of purchasing the participatory interest (or part of a participatory interest) in the statutory fund should distribute the participatory interest (or part of the participatory interest) between all participants of the company or should sell the participatory interest (part of the participatory interest) in accordance with the pre-emption right (Article 100 of the Law on Companies).

[265] If these persons decline to buy the share, the participant has the right to sell it to a third party or parties provided the company's charter does not prohibit its

sale to third parties (Articles 98, 99 of the Law on Companies). In such cases, alienation of the participatory interest (part of the participatory interest) in the statutory fund of the company to third parties is carried out at the price and subject to the conditions proposed to the participants and to the company (Article 101 of the Law on Companies).

[266] If the participants rejected their pre-emption rights, and the company declined to acquire the participatory interest, a sale and purchase agreement in respect of the participatory interest in the statutory fund is concluded with a third party.

[267] The company must be notified in writing of the alienation of the participatory interest (or part of a participatory interest) in the company's statutory fund with submission of proofs of such alienation. The purchaser of the participatory interest (part of participatory interest) of the company exercises the rights and performs the participant's duties from the date of notification of the company of the above-mentioned alienation (Article 101 of the Law on Companies).

[268] Then, changes in the charter due to changes in the composition of the participants are made and registered. The deadline for making changes to the charter and submitting it for state registration is two months (paragraph 22 of the State Registration Act).

2.6.8 Subsidiaries

[269] A subsidiary is not liable for the debts of the parent company. However, if a subsidiary is deemed insolvent (bankrupt) due to the parent company's fault, the parent company will be liable if and to the extent the subsidiary's property is insufficient to cover the debts (Article 7 of the Law on Companies).

2.6.9 Liability of a Company and Its Participants/Shareholders

[270] The Law on Companies sets out the main principles of the autonomy and limited liability of a company: the founder (participant) of a company is not liable for the company's obligations, and the company is not responsible for the participants' obligations unless otherwise provided by law or by the company's charter (Article 5 of the Law on Companies).

[271] The scope of liability of an LLC's participants and a joint-stock company's shareholders is similar.

[272] An LLC's participants and a joint-stock company's shareholders are generally not liable for the company's debts. Their risk of loss is limited to the value of the participatory interests/shares they own (Articles 71, 95 of the Law on Companies).

[273] Participants and shareholders who have not fully paid for their participatory interests or shares are jointly and severally liable for the liabilities of the company

to the extent of the unpaid portion of their participatory interests or shares (Articles 71, 95 of the Law on Companies).

[274] In addition, participants and shareholders may be liable for the debts of the company if their deliberate actions result in the insolvency or bankruptcy of the company (Article 5 of the Law on Companies).

[275] If the target company is in an insolvency procedure, various options are available. For example, the conclusion of a settlement agreement. A settlement agreement may be concluded on terms whereby the debtor's obligations are undertaken by a third party (Article 153 of the Economic Insolvency (Bankruptcy) Act).

2.6.10 Choice of Law

[276] Belarusian law generally recognises the choice of law, jurisdiction and arbitration clauses in contractual arrangements subject to the following.

[277] According to the Civil Code of Belarus, the parties to the contract may choose the applicable law, if the contract is concluded with the involvement of foreign citizens or foreign legal persons or is complicated by another foreign element.

[278] According to Decree No. 8, shareholder agreements (contracts) on the exercise of the rights of participants in limited (additional) liability companies may contain provisions on the application of foreign law to them, regardless of the presence of a foreign element in the transaction (including the citizenship (place of residence) of natural persons or the place of establishment (registration, place of activity) of legal persons).

[279] However, foreign law cannot be applied in cases where its application is contrary to the fundamentals of the law and order (the public procedure) of Belarus, as well as in other cases directly provided for by legislative acts. In these cases, the law of Belarus must be applied.

[280] Rules on the choice of law do not affect the imperative norms of the law of Belarus regulating the corresponding relations, regardless of the law which is being applied.

[281] It should be noted that if a Belarusian court is not able to ascertain the contents of the relevant law chosen by the parties within a reasonable time, it will apply Belarusian law.

[282] The rules on arbitrability need to be observed so that any award would be enforceable both in Belarus and in any country which is a party to the New York Convention.

[283] The parties to the agreement may agree to submit disputes arising out of the agreement to the courts of arbitration of a foreign jurisdiction.

2.7 Specific Rules on Public Takeovers

2.7.1 The Preemptive Right to Acquire the Ownership of the Respective Region, the City of Minsk Shares/Participatory Interests of Companies

[284] Regional executive committees and the Minsk City Executive Committee have a preemptive right to acquire the ownership of the relevant region, the city of Minsk shares/participatory interests of companies located in the territory of this region, the city of Minsk: (1) included in the lists of companies whose shares were purchased by citizens of Belarus for cash on preferential terms (at a price 20% below their nominal value) and (or) in exchange for personal privatisation checks 'Property', or received in exchange for shares of citizens in the property of rental and collective (people's) enterprises during their transformation into joint-stock companies in the course of privatisation; (2) created in the process of transformation of the state, state unitary, rental and collective (people's) enterprises, collective farms (agricultural PCs) (clause 1.4 of Edict of the President of Belarus dated 16 November 2006 No. 677).

[285] The lists of companies are posted on the information boards, and official websites of public bodies and are also made available through other accessible means, including media (agricultural PCs) (clause 1.5 of the Edict of the President of Belarus dated 16 November 2006 No. 677).

[286] If a shareholder/participant intends to sell shares/a participatory interest, they must send a notice by registered mail to the Regional Executive Committee, Minsk City Executive Committee specifying the sale price or place an application for the sale of shares on the Belarusian Currency and Stock Exchange. The Belarusian Currency and Stock Exchange informs the regional executive committees and the Minsk City Executive Committee daily about the placed bids for the sale of shares and share transactions (clause 1.4 of the Edict of the President of Belarus dated 16 November 2006 No. 677).

[287] The preemptive right to acquire shares/participatory interest does not apply in cases of: (1) donation of shares/participatory interest to close relatives and parents of a spouse; (2) transfer of ownership of shares/participatory interest in connection with the death of a participant; (3) exchange of shares/participatory interest during reorganisation; (4) redemption of shares of the company by the joint-stock company upon the request of its shareholders; (5) foreclosure of shares /participatory interest by court decision (clause 1.4 of the Edict of the President of Belarus dated 16 November 2006 No. 677).

[288] In the event of alienation of shares/participatory interest in violation of the preemptive right to acquire them, the regional executive committee, Minsk City Executive Committee has the right to claim before the court, within ninety calendar days, the transfer to them of the rights and obligations of the acquirer of such shares/participatory interest (clause 1.4 of the Edict of the President of Belarus dated 16 November 2006 No. 677).

2.8 Other Relevant Laws and Due Diligence Issues

2.8.1 Standards of Environmental, Social and Corporate Governance

[289] The National Action Plan for the Development of the 'Green Economy' for 2021–2025 is being implemented in Belarus. An interdepartmental working group has been established on the basis of the Ministry of Finance, which is working on the implementation of environmental, social and corporate governance (ESG) standards in Belarus.

[290] In 2023, the Government plans to adopt a resolution regulating the criteria and requirements for the verification system of projects and financial instruments of the 'green orientation'. The resolution will determine the criteria for 'green orientation' projects in such areas as waste management, energy, construction, industry, transport and others.

[291] BIK Ratings (the first and currently the only national rating agency accredited by the NB) has developed a unique methodology for assigning ESG ratings, which is based on international experience and includes an assessment of environmental, social and corporate risks of the company.

[292] In M&A transactions, the importance of compliance with ESG criteria by the target companies increases, since investors tend to asses non-financial risks of businesses. In legal due diligence, investors are often interested in the availability of option plans for employees, the availability of internal policies aimed at creating equal opportunities, and the absence of cases of harassment in the workplace.

2.8.2 Anti-bribery and Anti-corruption Laws; Money-Laundering Regulations

[293] In 2022, Transparency International ranked Belarus 91st out of 180 countries in its Corruption Perception Index. The main anti-bribery and anti-corruption laws which may affect M&A activity in Belarus are the Law 'On Combating Corruption', the Law 'On the Basics of Crime Prevention Activities', Decree of the President of Belarus 'On Strengthening the Requirements for Managerial Personnel and Employees of Organizations', Decree of the President of Belarus 'On Additional Measures to Combat Corruption', the Criminal Code and the Code on Administrative Offences. These laws envisage criminal and administrative liability for various categories of individuals, including, *inter alia*, state and local governmental officials, officers and employees of private companies and individuals. The majority of corruption crimes provide for liability in the form of imprisonment, deprivation of the right to hold certain positions or to engage in certain activities. Belarus has also ratified the United Nations (UN) Convention on Combating Corruption dated 14 December 2003.

[294] Anti-corruption measures are carried out by the entities of the Prosecutor's Office, internal affairs and State security of Belarus. The state entity responsible for

organising anti-corruption measures is the Prosecutor General's Office of Belarus. Specialised bodies for combating crime and corruption include:

- coordination meetings on combating crime and corruption (at the republican level headed by the Prosecutor General of Belarus);
- coordination meetings in the regions and Minsk;
- coordination meetings in districts, districts in cities, and cities;
- coordination meetings in the Armed Forces of Belarus, other troops and military formations.

[295] Within the structure of the State Control Committee of Belarus, the Financial Monitoring Department has been established. It is a financial monitoring body authorised in accordance with the legislation of Belarus to carry out activities to prevent the legalisation of proceeds from crime and the financing of terrorist activities. The Department has established and consistently operates an automated system for accounting, processing and analysing information on financial transactions subject to special control. The Department has established a working group to study typologies for the legalisation of illegal income which includes representatives of banks and law enforcement officials. Within the framework of international cooperation, information exchange is carried out with thirty-nine other states. According to international experts, the level of anti-money laundering in Belarus (at the legislative level) meets the international standards of the FATF (Financial Action Task Force on Money Laundering), which is an important condition for attracting funds from external investors.

[296] The maximum criminal penalty for money laundering according to the Criminal Code is ten years' imprisonment with a fine and with the deprivation of the right to hold certain positions or engage in certain activities.

2.8.3 Environmental Laws

[297] The law regulating environmental protection is the law 'On Environmental Protection'. The Water Code, the Land Code, the Subsurface Code, the Law 'On Wildlife' should also be taken into account. Environmental laws must be considered in the context of the acquisition of companies. Enterprises generally must obtain necessary licences and permits, and adhere to specific requirements, etc. It is important that legal consultants conducting the due diligence verify that all necessary licences and permits have been secured by the target and are in good standing.

2.8.4 Intellectual Property Rights

[298] According to the Law 'On Copyright and Related Rights', the objects of copyright are literary works (books, brochures, articles, etc.); dramatic and musical-dramatic works, works of choreography and pantomime, and other scripted works; musical works with and without text; audiovisual works (film, television, video, filmstrip, etc.); works of fine art (sculpture, painting, graphics, lithography, etc.); works of applied art and design; works of architecture, urban planning and landscape art; photographic works, including works obtained by methods similar to

photography; maps, plans, sketches, illustrations, and plastic works related to geography, cartography, and other sciences; computer programs; works of science (monographs, articles, reports, scientific lectures and reports, dissertations, design documentation, etc.) and other works. The objects of copyright also include derivative works and composite works.

[299] Copyright arises by virtue of the fact of its creation. No formalities are required for the creation and exercise of copyright.

[300] According to the Civil Code of Belarus, the right of industrial property extends to inventions; utility models; industrial designs; breeding achievements; integrated circuit topologies; production secrets (know-how); brand names; trademarks and service marks; geographical indications and other objects of industrial property.

[301] A trademark can be registered in various forms, including word marks, logos in any colour or colour combinations, packages, etc. Legal protection of trademarks in Belarus is carried out on the basis of their registration with the National Centre of Intellectual Property or in accordance with international agreements, in particular, the Madrid Agreement Concerning the International Registration of Marks and the Protocol relating to the Madrid Agreement on the International Registration of Marks.

[302] A trademark may be registered in the name of an organisation or an individual. Filing an application with the National Centre of Intellectual Property, conducting business with the National Centre of Intellectual Property can be carried out by the applicant independently or through a patent attorney registered in the National Intellectual Property Centre. It is obligatory for applicants who have a permanent place of residence or permanent residence in foreign countries, or their foreign patent attorneys, to conduct cases related to the application and registration of trademarks in Belarus through Belarusian patent attorneys, unless otherwise provided by international treaties of Belarus.

[303] Registration of a trademark in Belarus may take up to two years but actually takes an average of twelve months. The validity period of the registration and the period for which it is extended is ten years. The number of renewals is unlimited.

[304] The term of validity of a patent in Belarus for an invention is twenty years from the date of filing the application, subject to payment of annual fees. If the use of the means in which the invention is used requires the permission of the authorised body in accordance with the law, the validity period of the patent for such an invention is extended by the patent body upon the request of the patent owner for a period of not more than five years.

[305] Generally, assessment of intangible assets is required when solving a specific task and is determined by the purpose of use. In practice, the problem of assessing intangible assets arises in connection with the sale and purchase of rights to these objects, compulsory licensing and determination of damages resulting from infringement of rights.

The difficulty of assessment lies in the following:

(1) intangible assets are not always clearly defined. When assessing them, it is necessary to correctly classify the object. For example, it is not always clear what the notion of a brand includes. It may consist of trademark, trade name, reputation, and so on;

(2) it is not clear how to determine the value of the asset. For a practical assessment of the cost, there are several approaches:

    (a) costly (the value is determined by the sum of the costs of creating, acquiring and putting into circulation);

    (b) profitable (the level of the current value of the advantages of using, which is quite a subjective belief); and

    (c) comparative (according to data of recent transactions with similar intangible assets; however this data is often confidential).

(3) it is difficult to quantify the results of the commercial use of intangible assets.

2.8.5 Agency Agreements and Distribution Agreements

[306] The agency agreement and the distribution agreement are not directly named in the law of Belarus. However, their conclusion and determination of key provisions are possible in accordance with the principle of freedom of contract.

2.8.6 'Change of Control' Clauses

[307] 'Change of control' clauses are commonly used in banking credit agreements. Typically, such agreements require the target company to notify the bank of changes in its shareholder structure. In the event of a change in control, banks, as a rule, can demand, at their discretion, an early repayment of the loan or the provision of additional security for obligations, if they deem it necessary.

2.9 The Due Diligence Process

[308] Nowadays a due diligence process precedes most M&A deals involving a functioning business in Belarus. Due diligence can be either external, carried out at the initiative of the investor before making a decision to conclude a deal, or internal.

[309] External due diligence: by acquiring a share or shares of a company, an investor acquires its history. He will therefore want, so far as possible, to guard against risks associated with various kinds of violations or omissions in the company's activities from the moment of its creation to the moment the investor enters the company. In addition, by getting acquainted with the results of the due diligence, the investor receives detailed information about the structure of the

business, the specifics of the company's activities and its relations with customers and suppliers, as well as with governmental agencies. This enables the investor to understand the processes within the acquired company, assess its potential, and more accurately plan the direction and volume of investments.

[310] Internal due diligence (also known as vendor due diligence) is initiated by the company itself, when it wishes to prepare optimally for an upcoming full or partial sale and to identify and correct any existing shortcomings in advance. Despite the fact that internal due diligence is usually carried out in anticipation of the sale of a share to an investor, some companies carry out periodic checks, based on the results of which decisions are made to improve the management of the company.

[311] As a rule, the following issues are checked during legal due diligence:

- corporate matters: incorporation documents, the statutory fund, reorganisations, management systems, powers of attorney, registered office and rents, records of affiliates;
- intellectual property: the company's rights to intangible assets, formalisation of intellectual property rights with regard to counterparties;
- labour: formalisation of trade secrets regime, employee contracts, formalisation of intellectual property rights with regard to employees;
- general commercial issues, including contracts with customers. With regard to immovable property, it is normal to obtain certificates of title;
- regulatory issues (for instance, licences/permits);
- personal data protection;
- disputes and litigation: current litigation involving the company (whether on the side of the plaintiff, the defendant, or third parties), court decisions issued with regard to claims against the company that have not been enforced yet.

[312] Separate financial and tax due diligence may also be conducted. Ecological due diligence is uncommon (it may be conducted with regard to manufacturing enterprises). With the growing interest in sustainable investing, ESG standards are often covered within legal due diligence.

[313] Before conducting due diligence, it is common to form a data room – an information room containing all the documents to be checked. In some cases, the physical transfer of documents takes place – when the original documents are placed in subject folders and collected on the premises of the seller or transferred to the buyer's representatives. However, the most convenient and widespread method in practice, especially among IT companies, is the formation of a virtual information room. All documents are scanned and either transferred to the buyer's representatives on a flash drive or other material carrier, or more often are placed in a cloud storage, to which access is provided for the team of lawyers conducting the due diligence. The data room is filled in accordance with the list of documents requested by the buyer, or by the team of internal lawyers (in the case of vendor due diligence). This list is usually quite extensive and covers all areas of the company's operations.

[314] Judging from our own practice, it is crucial to negotiate with the client the following issues to make sure that you are on the same page and that your expectations are the same:

- to negotiate the scope of the due diligence, for instance, to specify whether you will conduct only legal due diligence or other types of due diligence as well (e.g., tax due diligence);
- whether the due diligence will be conducted entirely or only selectively and if selectively, what will be the criteria for such selection;
- the main risks (so-called red flags) should also be discussed with the client, since it is important to understand which assets are indeed important for the client and which risks he is trying to neutralise;
- the type of the report is another key issue since the report may specify only key risks (a 'red flags' report) or may contain descriptive elements as well.

[315] Finally, the list of requested documents should be considered, generally thorough but reasonable. The target company may be unable to cope if the list of requested documents is too overwhelming.

[316] If specific risks are revealed during the due diligence, then there are several possible options for the development of events. Most likely the investor will demand to reduce the price of the company, or impose on the seller an obligation to eliminate the revealed shortcomings.

[317] The most popular means of protecting the investor are through representations, warranties and indemnities. The possibility of using such mechanisms is granted to residents of the HTP by virtue of Decree No. 8.

[318] Representations and warranties are statements of fact that are significant to the buyer. Usually, the buyer provides two large groups of representations and warranties: in relation to himself (the existence of rights to conclude a transaction and rights in relation to the company) and in relation to the company being sold (e.g., the absence of encumbrances on assets, reliability of reporting, etc.). This list is not limited and depends on the identified risks.

[319] In accordance with Decree No. 8, the parties may stipulate in the contract liability for the inaccuracy of representations and warranties in the form of: indemnities, fines or unilateral termination of the agreement. The investor's right to unilaterally terminate the agreement is in line with normal market practice and should not be a matter of serious concern, but the grounds for exercising, it must be limited to the falsity of a few fundamental representations and warranties. In addition to these consequences, the parties may agree on others, for example, the buyer's right to exercise a put option or a call option, the redistribution of rights and obligations under the shareholder's agreement (e.g., the termination of rights to receive dividends or the limitation of the right to nominate candidates to the governing bodies).

[320] It will be in the interests of the seller to determine the limit of indemnities, for example, by reference to the aggregate consideration to be received. In addition, the amount of indemnities may be reduced by the court if it is proved that the

investor intentionally or due to gross negligence contributed to the increase of liability, or did not take reasonable measures to minimise it.

[321] The seller can reduce or even eliminate the risk of liability for the inaccuracy of representations and warranties by means of a disclosure letter, in which the seller may disclose to the buyer any inconsistencies with specific representations before signing the agreement. In such cases, the representations are interpreted taking into account the inconsistencies disclosed in the letter. At first glance, it seems that it would be more logical to simply exclude such assurances. In fact, the representations are usually broadly worded and cover a number of issues in respect of which they continue to operate. First, the disclosure letter will normally indicate public resources, information which is available to the buyer. It is in the interests of the seller to leave this list open, and in the interests of the buyer – to limit it. Further, the disclosure letter will list any representations which cannot be made and will detail the reasons for this.

[322] It should be borne in mind that often the seller's liability is unlimited in case of falsity of the most important (fundamental) representations.

2.10 Role of the Courts

[323] In general, individual and corporate shareholders, as well as nationals and foreigners have equal rights before the courts. Therefore, we do not see any potential prejudices or biases on the part of the courts in this regard. However, in labour disputes, the courts tend to support employees more often than the employer.

[324] Unfortunately, there is as yet no judicial practice or precedent on corporate disputes, including disputes arising from shareholder agreements and the provisions enshrined in them, such as restrictive covenants, confidentiality constraints, protection of minority shareholder rights and enforcement of warranty or indemnity claims, between foreign investors and other shareholders.

2.10.1 Economic Courts

[325] Economic cases are examined in the first instance by regional economic courts and the Minsk City Economic Court. Some cases are examined in the first instance by the Supreme Court of Belarus (cases involving state secrets, appeals against non-normative acts of national state bodies, etc.). In addition, the Supreme Court of Belarus is entitled to initiate proceedings in, and to assume the jurisdiction of, any case as a Court of First Instance.

[326] Economic Courts of First Instance normally proceed in two main stages:

(1) preparation of a case for proceedings (which results in a preparatory court hearing within no more than fifteen working days from the date of receipt of the suit by the court);

(2) court proceedings.

[327] As a general rule, a case is examined by a court within two months at most from the date of adoption of a court ruling on the assignment of the case for judicial examination. Thus, a dispute between Belarusian residents will be adjudicated in a Court of First Instance within at most three months (including the time required to prepare the case).

[328] Some cases (disputes on state property, connected with state registration and liquidation of legal entities and IEs; disputes on the release of distrained property) are examined within one month from the date of adoption of a court ruling on the assignment of the case for judicial examination.

[329] Cases on certain kinds of proceedings (cases appealing against non-regulatory acts, actions (inaction) of state bodies, cases on recognition and enforcement of decisions issued by foreign courts and foreign arbitral awards) are examined within at most one month from the date of receipt of application (complaint) by the economic court.

[330] A case involving a foreign entity located outside Belarus will be examined by an Economic Court of First Instance within at most seven months from the date of adoption of a court ruling on the assignment of the case for judicial examination, unless otherwise specified by a corresponding international treaty of Belarus.

[331] However, if management bodies of foreign entities, their branches, representative offices or representatives authorised to participate in the case are located within the territory of Belarus, cases involving such foreign entities are examined within generally prescribed time frames.

[332] In exceptional cases, with due account for the special complexity of a case, a period for a case to be examined may be extended by the chairperson of an economic court or by his/her deputy for up to four months, and for a case involving a foreign entity located outside Belarus – up to twelve months.

2.10.2 Arbitration

[333] Apart from national courts, disputes may also be resolved by international arbitration courts (IACs).

[334] Legal relations connected with the establishment and activities of IACs in Belarus are regulated by Law No. 279-Z 'On International Arbitration/Mediation Courts' dated 9 July 1999.

[335] A dispute may be resolved in a permanent IAC or in an ad hoc IAC.

[336] Two permanent IACs operating in Belarus are:

- the IAC under the Belarusian Chamber of Commerce and Industry (BelCCI);
- the international arbitration/mediation court 'Chamber of Arbitrators under the Lawyers Union'.

3 MERGER CONTROLS: ANTITRUST/ COMPETITION ISSUES

3.1 Relevant Legislation and Competent Authorities

[337] The antimonopoly legislation of Belarus is as follows:

– Law of Belarus No. 94-Z dated 12 December 2013 'On Suppression of Monopolistic Activity and Development of Business Competition' and Law of Belarus No. 162-Z dated 16 December 2002 'On Natural Monopolies' regulating monopolistic activity.
– Edict of the President of Belarus No. 385 'On the creation and activities of holdings companies' dated 7 October 2021 regulating the creation and activities of holding companies.
– Instruction 'On Determination of Dominant (Monopsony) Position of Business Entities' approved by Resolution of the Ministry of Antimonopoly Regulation and Trade of Belarus No. 63 dated 27 December 2017, prescribing the rules to be used to determine a dominant position of a business entity in a particular commodity market.
– 'Regulation of the Administrative Procedure to be Carried Out in Relation to Business Entities' under Sub-Clause 2.8.4 'Obtaining a Document of Approval to Acquire Capital Stocks (Shares) of a Business Entity', approved by Resolution No. 11 of the Ministry of Antimonopoly Regulation and Trade of Belarus No. 11 dated 31 January 2022, describes the procedure for obtaining approval to acquire capital stocks (shares) and contains a list of documents that must be submitted in order to obtain such approval.
– 'Regulation of the Administrative Procedure to be Carried out in Relation to Business Entities' under Sub-Clause 2.8.3 'Obtaining a Document of Approval to Establish a Holding Company, Inclusion of a Business Entity into the Members of Holding', describes the procedure for obtaining approval to the establishment of a holding company, the inclusion in the holding company, and contains a list of documents that must be submitted in order to obtain such approval.

[338] The antimonopoly authority – the Ministry of Antimonopoly Regulation and Trade of Belarus and its structural subdivisions – the main departments of the Ministry of Antimonopoly Regulation and Trade of Belarus in regions and Minsk city implement antimonopoly policies in Belarus.

[339] An approval of the antimonopoly authority must be obtained before implementation of an M&A transaction or submitting documents to register a holding company where such approval is required. In certain cases, an approval of the antimonopoly authority is not mandatory. Instead, a written notification must be sent to the antimonopoly authority within one month of the date of the transaction, or registering a holding company, or including a new company in the existing holding.

3.2 Scope of the Controls

3.2.1 Transactions with Capital Stocks (Shares)

[340] Approval of the antimonopoly authority is required for a transaction with capital stocks (shares) where:

- the total balance sheet value of assets of the entity selling capital stocks (shares) or of the entity buying capital stocks (shares) as of the latest reporting date exceeds 200 000 basic units; or
- where total revenues from sales of goods (works, services) of the entity selling capital stocks (shares) or of the entity buying capital stocks (shares) in the reporting year immediately preceding the year of acquisition exceed 400 000 basic units (excluding VAT); or
- where one of such business entities is included in the State Register of business entities with a dominant position in the commodity markets or in the State Register of natural monopolies.

[341] A transaction corresponding to one of the above-mentioned criteria is subject to the approval of the antimonopoly body when it results in:

(1) acquisition of a right to dispose of a block of capital stocks (shares):
   (a) of more than 25% of capital stocks (shares), if the acquirer was not previously a participant in such business entity, or had a share of 25% or less;
   (b) of more than 50% of capital stocks (shares), if previously the acquirer had a share of 25% to 50% in such business entity.
(2) acquisition of, in total, over 25% of capital stocks (shares) of another business entity in a particular commodity market by a business entity holding a dominant position in the same commodity market;
(3) acquisition by a business entity of at least 25% of the capital stocks (shares) of a business entity holding a dominant position in a commodity market, or other transactions enabling such acquirer to influence the decision-making process of such business entity holding a dominant position in a commodity market.

[342] An approval of the antimonopoly authority to conclude a transaction is not required in the following cases:

(1) if the transaction is to be concluded by a business entity (partnership) or an individual or a business entity, if the latter due to its participation in such business entity (partnership) or in accordance with the powers received from other persons (including under an agreement) already has more than 50% of the total number of capital stocks (shares) of such business entity (partnership);

(2) the acquirer and the business entity whose capital stocks (shares) are being acquired have the same persons holding more than 50% of the votes attributable to the capital stocks (shares);

(3) capital stocks (shares) are transferred to a professional securities market participant for trust management, as well as if the transfer of capital stocks (shares) is carried out in the framework of implementation of the requirements of the legislation on public service and legislation on anticorruption;

(4) a business entity acquires capital stocks (shares) fund of itself (buy-back);

(5) capital stocks (shares) are acquired by the founders during the establishment of the business entity.

In such a case, the legislation establishes the obligation to notify the antimonopoly authority in writing within one month from the effective date of the transaction.

[343] Failure to obtain an approval of the antimonopoly authority for a transaction with capital stocks (shares) of a business entity and any transactions resulting in the establishment or reinforcement of a dominant position in a commodity market and/or in a limitation of business competition will entail invalidation of such transaction by court.

[344] Non-compliance with this obligation will not of itself cause invalidation. The essential condition is the fact that a transaction has resulted in the establishment or reinforcement of a dominant position of a business entity in a commodity market and/or in limitation of competition. However, this fact must be proved in court.

3.2.2 Creation of Holding Companies

[345] Before submitting documents to register a holding company, an interested party must obtain an approval of the antimonopoly authority for the creation of such a holding company where:

(1) the total balance sheet value of the assets of the business entities forming such holding company, estimated on the basis of financial statements as of the latest reporting date, exceeds 200 000 basic units; or

(2) the total revenues of the business entities forming such holding company from sales of goods in the reporting year immediately preceding the year of creation of the holding company exceed 400 000 (excluding VAT) basic units; or

(3) one such entity is included in the State Register of business entities with a dominant position in the commodity markets of Belarus or in the State Register of natural monopolies.

The approval of the antimonopoly authority for the inclusion of a business entity in a holding company is always required regardless of any criteria.

3.3 Process/Mechanics

[346] To start the procedure, the application must be submitted to the antimonopoly authority. In the case of acquisitions of capital stocks (shares), the application must be accompanied by the following documents and information:

- copies of the balance sheet (with the profit and loss account) of both the acquirer and the target business entity approved as of the date preceding the submission of the application;
- information on the main types of activity, goods (works, services), production volumes, supplies to Belarus and export of goods in kind and in value terms of both the acquirer and the target business entity;
- the list of persons belonging to the same group as the acquirer and the target business entity separately. If persons belonging to the same group of persons operate in the same commodity market as the acquirer or target, information on the main types of activity of the goods (works, services), production volumes, supplies to Belarus and export of goods in kind and in value terms of such persons shall be provided in addition;
- the draft document formalising the transaction as of the date preceding the date of submission of the application;
- information on the main types of activity, goods (works, services), production volumes, supplies to Belarus and export of goods in kind and in value terms of both the acquirer and the target business entity.

In the case of establishing (incorporating) a holding company, the application must be accompanied by the following documents and information:

- A copy of the resolution establishing (incorporating) a holding company.
- Information on the main types of activity, goods (works, services), production volumes, supplies to Belarus and export of goods in kind and in value terms of both each member of the holding company (if established) or each member of the holding company and the business entity included in the holding company (if incorporated).
- The list of persons belonging to the same group as each of the holding company members (or each of the holding company members and the business entity included in the holding company). If persons belonging to the same group of persons operate in the same commodity market as the holding company members or the holding company members and the business entity included in the holding company, information on the main types of activity of the goods (works, services), production volumes, supplies to Belarus and export of goods in kind and in value terms of such persons shall be provided in addition.

If the member of the holding company (the person included in the member of the holding company) or if the acquirer is a non-resident of Belarus, the following documents shall be submitted in addition:

- An extract from the commercial register of the country of establishment or other equivalent proof of the legal status of the foreign organisation under the legislation of the country of its establishment (requires legalisation and notarised translation into Belarusian or Russian). The excerpt should be dated one year before the date of application.
- A document confirming state registration of a branch or representative office (if there are branches or representative offices registered in Belarus) (requires legalisation and notarised translation into Belarusian or Russian).

[347] Within ten working days of receiving the application and documents, the antimonopoly authority shall decide to refuse to accept it if the documents and/or information are not submitted or do not meet the established requirements. If the documents and information comply with the requirements, the antimonopoly authority must render its decision within thirty days from the date of application (ten working days are included in thirty days). The antimonopoly authority may:

- either approve the establishing a holding company (inclusion in the holding company) or acquiring capital stocks (shares); or
- render a substantiated decision declining the approval, if a transaction in capital stocks (shares) or the establishing a holding company (inclusion in the holding company) may lead to the establishment or reinforcement of a dominant position in a commodity market and/or a limiting, eliminating or preventing of business competition, or if, during the application process, the antimonopoly authority discovers that the submitted information is inaccurate and/or incomplete.

[348] The antimonopoly authority may approve a transaction in capital stocks (shares) or establish a holding company (inclusion in the holding company) even if it entails reinforcement of a dominant position in a commodity market and/or if business competition is thereby limited, eliminated or prevented. To obtain such a decision, the business entities have to prove that their actions have or may have the following effects:

- they improve production, sales of goods (works, services), or stimulate technical (economic) progress, or increase the competitiveness of goods (works, services) manufactured in Belarus in the global commodity market;
- consumers receive advantages (benefits) proportionate to the advantages (benefits) acquired by the corresponding business entities due to such actions.

[349] The antimonopoly authority's approval is valid for one year.

[350] Failure to submit an application for approval of a transaction may be deemed as failure to present data (documents, explanations), enabling the antimonopoly authority to discharge their functions (in terms of monitoring economic concentration), which may entail a fine in the amount of up from 20 to 100 basic units in accordance with the Administrative Violations Code.

3.4 Anti-competitive Restraints

3.4.1 Non-compete Agreement

[351] Decree No. 8 has provided new legal instruments as non-compete and non-solicitation clauses that can be used by residents of the HTP.

[352] Where a non-compete agreement is intended to be concluded by a resident of the HTP and its employee. In accordance with Decree No. 8, a non-compete agreement is an agreement stipulating that an employee must willingly (for a stipulated compensation) undertake, for a specific period of time stipulated therein, to refrain from concluding any employment and/or civil law contracts/agreements with third parties which are competitors of a given HTP resident, and/or must undertake to refrain from any independent non-corporate competitive business activities, or refrain from acting as a founder/participant of any entity competing with a given HTP resident, or refrain from acting as CEO or board member of such competing entity.

[353] This kind of agreement is concluded as a separate document or as a clause in an employment agreement/contract.

[354] Such agreements involve the following essential conditions:

- compensation to be paid to the employee for each month he/she abides by the terms of the non-compete agreement, after termination of employment relationship. Compensation paid after the termination of such employee's employment relationship cannot be lower than the established minimum limit – at least one-third of the average monthly earnings during the last year of employment;
- the duration of the non-compete agreement may cover the entire period of the employment relationship, but cannot last for more than one year after termination of the employee's employment relationship;
- specification of the particular business activity covered by the non-compete agreement;
- specification of the territory covered by the non-compete agreement.

3.4.2 Non-solicitation Agreement

[355] A non-solicitation agreement is used in order to prohibit companies from soliciting employees from each other. Such agreements may involve an HTP resident and any company, even a non-resident of Belarus.

[356] A non-solicitation agreement is an agreement providing that one party will compensate losses caused to the other party upon demand and/or will pay a forfeit or penalty stipulated by such agreement, should one of the parties (or an affiliated person of one of the parties) commit an action resulting in termination of the employment relationship between the other party and its employee(s) and the establishment of employment relations between such employee(s) and the first party (or an affiliated person of the first party).

[357] Such agreements are concluded by way of a separate document or as a clause in an ongoing agreement between the parties (for instance, as a clause in a consulting agreement or other form of services agreement).

[358] Such agreements involve the following essential conditions:

(1) scope (actions deemed to involve solicitation). In this context, parties concluding a non-solicitation agreement must realise or at least contemplate how alleged solicitation actions can be proven;
(2) liability for solicitation. Decree No. 8 stipulates the following types of eventual contractual liability:
    (a) losses established as liability regardless of whether specified or not in the non-solicitation agreement;
    (b) a forfeit /penalty, where stipulated by the non-solicitation agreement (which may be of any amount).

[359] By this means losses and/or forfeit penalties may be claimed under a non-solicitation agreement either separately or jointly. Furthermore, liability for an employee solicitation may apply not only to the party to the agreement but to its affiliated persons as well.

[360] It is advisable for the parties to a non-solicitation agreement to stipulate an effective period of duration of the agreement, although such clause is not an essential condition of a non-solicitation agreement (i.e., its absence doesn't invalidate it). Decree No. 8 does not specify an upper limit for the effective period of a non-solicitation agreement.

3.4.3 Agreements and Coordinated Actions

[361] Antimonopoly legislation prohibits agreements and coordinated actions of business entities if such agreements or coordinated actions result or may result in the prevention, limitation or elimination of business competition, including (but not limited to) the following agreements:

- imposing contractual clauses on sellers/consumers that are uneconomic or superfluous/irrelevant;
- establishing economically, technologically or otherwise unreasonable different prices/tariffs for the same product;
- involving the restriction of access to, withdrawal from, or exclusion of other business entities from a commodity market.

[362] Moreover, where the parties to such agreement are business competitors, agreements/arrangements between them are prohibited if they entail or may entail:

- establishing, increasing, decreasing or fixing prices (tariffs);
- division of a commodity market on a territory basis, by types/volumes of transactions, or by types/volumes/range of products and/or respective prices/tariffs, or by scope of sellers/consumers;

- reduction or termination of production of goods (works, services);
- refusal to conclude agreements with certain sellers/consumers, where such refusal is not stipulated by legislative acts.

[363] Moreover, the antimonopoly law provides for specific rules in respect of 'vertical agreements', i.e., agreements involving a business entity acquiring goods or acting as a potential purchaser, and another business entity providing goods or acting as a potential seller.

[364] The antimonopoly law forbids vertical agreements:

- where such agreements lead or may lead to an establishment of a resale price of a product, except for cases where the seller fixes a maximum resale price for a buyer;
- where such agreements provide for the buyer's obligation not to sell any goods of a business entity competing with the seller. This prohibition does not apply to agreements on the consumer's organisation of sale of goods under the seller's/manufacturer's trademark or another identification mark.

[365] Agreements and coordinated actions may be considered acceptable by the antimonopoly authority (except for prohibited agreements between competitors), if they do not impose on other business entities any restrictions irrelevant for the purposes thereof and do not entail or enable prevention, restriction or elimination of competition in the relevant commodity market, providing the business entities concerned can prove one of the following consequences:

- improvement of production (sales) of goods, or stimulation of technical (economic) progress, or increase in the competitiveness in the global commodity market of goods manufactured in Belarus;
- consumers receive a proportionate share of the advantages (benefits) acquired by the entities concerned as a result of such actions.

[366] Vertical agreements are allowed:

- if such agreements are complex business licence agreements (franchising agreements);
- if the share of each business entity party to such agreement in any commodity market does not exceed 20%.

3.4.4 A Dominant Position

[367] A 'dominant position' of a business entity is determined in accordance with the legislation of Belarus based on an analysis of the relevant commodity market conducted by the antimonopoly authority of Belarus. The Instruction 'On Determination of Dominant (Monopsony) Position of Business Entities approved by Resolution of the Ministry of Antimonopoly Regulation and Trade of Belarus' No. 63 dated 27 December 2017 prescribes the rules to be used to determine a dominant position of a business entity in a particular commodity market.

The dominant position depends on the number of major competitors and the market shares:

- if there are 4–5 major competitors and each has a market share exceeding 15%, and together they together have a market share exceeding 75%, and during at least one year their market shares are invariable or subject to insignificant changes, as well as the access of new competitors to the respective commodity market is complicated; or
- if there are 2–3 major competitors and each has a market share exceeding 15% and together they together have a market share exceeding 50%, and during at least one year, their market shares are invariable or subject to insignificant changes, as well as the access of new competitors to the respective commodity market is complicated; or
- if there is one dominant business entity and (a) its market share is equal to or exceeds 35%, or (b) its market share exceeds 15% and the business entity is considered as dominant based on the discretion of antimonopoly authority.

Business entities holding a dominant position are included in the State Register of business entities with dominant position in the commodity markets of Belarus.

[368] For the purposes of identification of a business entity holding a dominant position, the following factors/characteristics will be taken into account:

- such business entity has no competitors in the corresponding commodity market;
- such business entity, although not being the only manufacturer (supplier) or consumer of a particular type of goods is, however, capable of imposing unacceptable terms of sale/purchase when executing the supply contract;
- such business entity is capable of limiting business competition by other business entities in the resource market (the market for raw/primary materials, equipment, energy resources, etc.);
- such business entity is capable of decreasing or limiting the supply of goods to the market in order to gain unilateral advantages, when executing the supply contract.

[369] If the position of a business entity (or several business entities) in a market is recognised as a dominant position, then production output, price levels and other indicators of such business entity (entities) will be subject to special government control aimed at preventing and restraining any abuse of such dominant position (if any).

[370] The activities of companies holding a dominant position in the commodity markets of Belarus are controlled by means of audits conducted by the antimonopoly authorities and by means of agreements stipulating compulsory terms and conditions excluding monopolistic activities and price/tariff ranges.

[371] Government bodies monitor the level of prices (tariffs) for goods (works, services) provided by business entities with market share dominance by means of setting fixed or limit prices (tariffs) or declaration of prices (tariffs) or prices (tariffs) indexation.

[372] The Administrative Violations Code provides for liability of officials of business entities in the amount of up from 20 to 100 basic units where such business entity holding a dominant position commits any act of abuse of its dominant position as specified by the antimonopoly law; for IEs, a fine of up from 100 to 200 basic units is prescribed, and for business entities – a fine of up to 10% of revenues from sales of goods (works, services) within the calendar year immediately preceding the year in which the administrative offence was identified, (or within a portion of the calendar year in which such administrative offence was detected immediately preceding the date of detection of such offence, if the offender was not involved in the sale of goods (works, services) in the preceding calendar year); however, the fine will be not less than 500 basic units.

4 TAXATION ASPECTS

4.1 Nature of the Tax Regime

[373] The Tax Code of Belarus (comprising the General Part and the Special Part) is the principal legal act regulating the system of taxes and duties levied on the national and local budgets, the main principles of taxation in Belarus, the official relations pertaining to the introduction, alteration and termination of taxes and duties, and relations arising in the course of discharge of tax liabilities, administration of tax control, appealing against orders of tax authorities, actions/inaction of tax officers, as well as establishing the rights and obligations of taxpayers, tax authorities and other participants of tax relations.

[374] The General Part specifies the notions of taxation elements. It also contains regulations on transfer pricing, tax accounting, control and describes the procedure for appealing decisions taken by tax authorities. The Special Part regulates the procedure for calculating and paying specific taxes and levies, objects of taxation, tax bases, tax rates, tax periods and tax benefits.

[375] All tax payments applicable in Belarus are subdivided into national taxes/duties and local taxes/duties.

4.2 Liability to Tax

[376] According to the Tax Code organisations that are payers of taxes, fees (duties) are understood as:

- legal entities of Belarus;
- foreign and international organisations, including those that are not legal entities;
- simple partnerships (participants in an agreement on joint activities, except for participants in an agreement on consortium lending).

[377] A Belarusian organisation (an organisation whose location is within the territory of Belarus) has the status of a tax resident of Belarus and fulfils tax obligations in respect of income from sources in Belarus, income from sources outside Belarus, as well as in respect of property located both on the territory of Belarus and outside it.

[378] A foreign organisation (an organisation whose location is not within the territory of Belarus) is not a tax resident of Belarus and fulfils tax obligations only in respect of activities carried out in Belarus, or in respect of income from sources in Belarus, as well as in respect of property located within the territory of Belarus. The location of an organisation (with the exception of a simple partnership) is generally recognised as the place of its state registration.

[379] If a representative office or other separate subdivision of a legal entity, in accordance with the accounting policy, maintains accounting records with the determination of the financial result of their activities, and if such a subdivision has an account opened for transactions by a legal entity with the right to dispose of funds to their officials, then they calculate the amount of taxes, dues (duties) and fulfil the tax obligations of a legal entity in terms of their activities, unless otherwise established by the Tax Code.

[380] An organisation or an individual recognised as a permanent establishment of a foreign organisation is obliged to:

– perform the tax obligations of such foreign organisation, as well as bear responsibility for their performance as established for payers and tax agents;
– pay taxes, fees (duties) at the expense of the funds of the foreign organisation of which they are a permanent establishment (VAT, profit tax, withholding tax, personal income tax, etc.) and if they are not enough and there are no other assets of the foreign organisation – at the expense of own funds.

4.3 Main Taxes

[381] Under the general taxation regime, the following taxes apply to Belarusian resident organisations, as well as foreign non-resident organisations that operate in Belarus through a permanent establishment or receive income from Belarusian sources.

[382] National taxes/duties:

– value added tax (VAT);
– excise duties;
– profit tax;
– tax on income of foreign entities having no permanent representative office in Belarus;
– personal income tax (as a tax agent);
– property tax;
– land tax;

- ecological tax;
- mineral extraction tax;
- offshore duty;
- stamp duty;
- consular fee;
- state duties;
- patent fees;
- customs fees and duties;
- waste disposal fee;
- transport tax;
- duty for placement (distribution) of advertisement.

[383] Local taxes/duties:

- packer shipper levy.

[384] Alongside the general taxation system, a simplified taxation system and specific regimes of taxation (e.g., High-Tech Park; Entrepreneurial activity on the territory of medium, small towns and rural areas; Great Stone Industrial Park) are also applied in Belarus. They provide a number of benefits, a lesser amount of assessed/paid taxes, reduced tax rates, etc.

Profit Tax

[385] Gross profits as well as dividends and similar incomes gained by Belarusian entities are items on which profit tax is levied.

[386] The gross profit of a Belarusian entity is the sum of profits from the sales of goods (works, services), property rights and non-sale incomes, decreased by the sum of non-sale expenses.

[387] The standard profit tax rate in Belarus is 20%.

[388] The 12% tax rate is applied to dividends accrued and paid to Belarusian entities (in some cases – 6% or 0%).

[389] The 10% rate is applied to profits of scientific/technology parks, technology transfer centres, residents of scientific/technology parks (except for profit tax calculated, withheld and paid by entities acting as tax agents).

[390] The 5% rate is applied to profits from sale of goods of own production, included in the list of high-tech goods, determined by the Council of Ministers of Belarus.

[391] The 25% rate is applied to profits of banks, insurance companies and forex companies from the activity of making transactions with non-deliverable OTC financial instruments.

[392] The 30% rate is applied to profits of operators of cellular mobile telecommunications, as well as profit of commercial microfinance organisations (until 1 January 2025).

Value Added Tax

[393] Belarus has several VAT rates, including 25%, 20%, 10%, 0% and the computed rate (for the retail trade).

[394] The 25% rate is applied to sales of telecommunication services.

[395] The 20% rate is the most frequently applied rate when selling goods, works, services, and property rights.

[396] The 10% rate is applied, for instance, to import and/or sales of food products and goods for children included in the List approved by the Tax Code, sales of agricultural production made in Belarus, import and/or sales of agricultural production made in other EAEU countries, import and/or sales of medicines and medical products.

[397] The 0% rate applies to sales of goods placed under the customs procedure of export and exported works for the production of goods from goods made on commission (materials) on condition documentary evidence of the factual export of such goods outside the territory of Belarus. This rate applies also to sales of exported transportation services, including transit transportation.

[398] VAT exemption is applied when importing electric cars into the territory of Belarus by legal entities if not more than five years have passed from the date of manufacture of such electric vehicles.

[399] Furthermore, the Tax Code allows application of a computed VAT rate for business entities focusing on retail trade and public catering.

Simplified Taxation System

[400] The simplified system of taxation can be applied only by organisations with incomes and the number of employees below a certain level, established by the legislation. Since 1 January 2023, individual entrepreneurs and notaries cannot apply the simplified system of taxation.

[401] Organisations that are legal entities of Belarus are entitled to use the simplified tax system in 2023, provided they comply with the following criteria:

- they have an average number of workers of not more than fifty persons during the first nine months of 2022;
- their accrued earnings during the first nine months of 2022 are not more than EUR500 (hereinafter based on the official exchange rate of 3.2 BYN per EUR).

[402] If gross proceeds of the organisation on an accrual basis during a calendar year exceed EUR670 and (or) the number of employees is more than fifty, the simplified tax system is not applied and taxes are paid according to the general procedure.

[403] The following organisations, in particular, do not have the right to apply the simplified taxation system:

(1) organisations that have one or more branches registered with the tax authorities;
(2) trustees and fiduciary managers in the fiduciary management of property;
(3) organisations exchanging digital signs (tokens) for other digital signs (tokens), disposing of digital signs (tokens) for electronic money, and receiving property (except for monetary assets in BYN and foreign currency) if such receipt is stipulated by operations with digital signs (tokens) or if the organisation has them;
(4) organisations receiving funds that do not constitute their gross proceeds in particular:
  – on the basis of commission, assignment or other similar civil law contracts, freight forwarding contracts;
  – as reimbursement (payment) of expenses irrespective of in whose interests they were made;
  – in connection with participation in settlements between other persons by receiving money from one person and transferring (transferring) it to another person.

[404] The tax base of tax under the simplified tax system is defined as monetary expression of gross proceeds. The gross proceeds are the sum of proceeds from sale of goods (work, services), proprietary rights and non-operating income. In accordance with the cash principle of revenue recognition, the tax base includes all receipts to the payer's account and cash, including prepayments (advances, deposits).

[405] The tax rate under the simplified taxation system is set at 6%.

[406] Under the simplified tax system, a large number of taxes are replaced by a single tax with a simplified calculation procedure.

[407] The tax under the simplified system substitutes the following taxes for corporate entities:

(1) Profit tax (except for taxes that are calculated, withheld and paid by entities acting as tax agents). The general procedure for paying profit tax is retained in some cases. For example:
  (a) dividends and profits accruing by a UE to its corporate founder;
  (b) profits of participants/shareholders of corporate entities in monetary form or in kind, resulting from the liquidation of a company or withdrawal of a membership, where such profit exceeds the capital contribution or actual expenses incurred/paid during the acquisition of a participatory share/stock;
  (c) profits of participants/shareholders of corporate entities in the form of value of a participatory/equity share/stock, as well as in the form of an increase of the par value of shares/stock produced on account of the company's own capital, where any member's/shareholder's participatory share changes by more than 0.01%;

(d) profits from selling bank bullion, weighted ingots or bullion coins made of precious metals to banks for a sum equal to a positive gain between the selling price and the acquisition price;

(e) a positive difference between the estimated value of property transferred by a taxpayer as a non-monetary contribution to the statutory fund of another taxpayer and the carrying value of such property;

(f) profits from sales/redemption of securities;

(g) profits from alienation/redemption of participatory/equity shares (or portions thereof) in economic entities;

(h) profits from sales of an enterprise as a property complex.

(2) VAT on overall sales of goods (works, services), and property rights.

The general procedure for the VAT still applies to the following cases:

(a) VAT on goods imported into Belarus.

(b) VAT on goods (work, services) and property rights sold in Belarus by foreign companies that do not operate in Belarus through a permanent establishment and are not registered with the Belarusian tax authorities.

(3) Real estate tax. The general procedure for real estate tax still applies to:

(a) permanent buildings/structures (or portions thereof) taken on (financial) lease or hired for other compensated or uncompensated usages;

(b) all taxable items of entities with a total area of permanent buildings/structures (or portions thereof) exceeding 1 000 m², provided they are in the ownership, economic control, operative management or (in certain cases) in usage, or on special file that is subject to state registration in case of (and prior to) creation/modification of the above-mentioned rights (where such registration is mandatory).

(4) Ecological tax, except for the ecological tax for the disposal of production wastes in case they acquire ownership of production wastes on the basis of a waste disposal transaction or other actions indicating the circulation of wastes in any other way for the purpose of subsequent disposal.

(5) Packer shipper levy.

4.4 Withholding Tax

[408] In Belarus, withholding tax is known as tax on revenues of foreign organisations having no permanent representative office in Belarus (hereinafter – 'revenue-based tax').

[409] The revenue-based tax is paid by foreign and international organisations (including non-legal entities) not operating in Belarus via a permanent representative office but deriving income from a source in Belarus.

[410] Corporate entities and IEs that assess and/or pay income to a foreign entity must compute and pay the revenue-based tax to the state budget. Such entities/

entrepreneurs are recognised as tax agents. In some cases, individuals are recognised as tax agents.

[411] The revenue-based tax applies to the following incomes:
- payment for transportation, freight, demurrage and other payments arising in transportation, in connection with the implementation of international transport, as well as payments for the provision of transport forwarding services;
- income on credits and loans;
- income from securities, where the terms of issue imply profit-making in the form of interest (discount);
- royalties;
- dividends and similar income;
- income from the sale of goods within the territory of Belarus under agency contracts, commission contracts and other similar civil law contracts;
- income from disposal of real estate situated in Belarus, or equity/ participatory shares (or portions thereof) of entities situated in Belarus;
- income from performed works/services, and other incomes of foreign organisations not operating in Belarus via a permanent representative office, as provided for by the Tax Code; where a specific type of income from works/ services is not specified by the Tax Code, it will not be regarded as an item subject to income tax.

[412] Tax rates depend on the type of income and may amount to 0%, 6%, 10%, 12% and 15%.

[413] The revenue-based tax rate on income from the alienation of a share in the statutory fund is set at 12%.

4.5 Double Tax Treaties

[414] In order to eliminate double taxation, Belarus has concluded a large number of bilateral agreements with other states. To date, such agreements have been concluded with more than seventy countries.

[415] A mandatory condition for the application of a double tax treaty is the provision by a foreign organisation of confirmation that it has a permanent location in the foreign state with which Belarus has concluded a double tax treaty. The confirmation must be certified by the competent authority of the relevant foreign state and may be provided in electronic form (it must contain an EDS and verification code).

[416] There are cases where the application of the income tax exemption requires that the foreign organisation is the actual (true) owner of the income. If the tax agent that accrues (pays) income doubts that a foreign organisation is the actual owner of income, it has the right to request documents (information) from such foreign organisation to confirm its status.

4.6 Tax Considerations Arising on M&A Transactions

[417] Transactions involving the sale of shares in the statutory fund or parts thereof are not subject to VAT. At the same time, the sale price does not matter. No Electronic VAT Invoice is needed to be created for such operations.

[418] Income from the sale of a share in the charter capital of an organisation is not sales revenue, but non-operating income.

[419] If the nominal value of the share was increased at the expense of the company's own capital, then in the event of a change in the percentage of participation in the statutory fund of the company of at least one of the participants by more than 0.01%, the participant's income in the form of the value of the shares of the same organisation is included in the expenses when determining the profit from the sale of the share. Such income is reflected on the date of the decision on the distribution (reallocation) of shares in the statutory fund.

[420] When taxing profits received from the sale of shares in the statutory fund of organisations located within the territory of Belarus, or part of them, the generally established income tax rate of 20% is applied.

[421] A foreign organisation that sells its share (or part of the share) in the statutory fund of a Belarusian organisation will be recognised as a revenue-based taxpayer, and the income received by a foreign organisation from the sale of the share will be recognised as an object of revenue-based tax.

[422] With regard to the calculation and payment of revenue-based tax, when selling a share in the statutory fund of a Belarusian organisation by a foreign legal entity (non-resident of Belarus), the need to actually revenue-based tax and transfer it to the budget is assigned to the organisation that acquires such share and carries out the duties of a tax agent.

4.7 Debt Financing

[423] Expenses related to a reorganisation are recognised as non-operating expenses and therefore reduce the tax base of profit tax.

4.8 Thin Capitalisation

[424] In Belarus, thin capitalisation rules have been applicable since 2013. In 2013 and 2014, they were applied only to interest on debt obligations paid to foreign organisations. Since 2015 the scope of the rules has expanded significantly.

[425] The thin capitalisation rules involve applying a restriction on the inclusion of certain types of expenses (interest; amounts of fines, penalties; costs of engineering, marketing, consulting, management and other services) in the costs (non-sale

expenses) taken into account for taxation. The specific debt/equity ratio is 3:1 generally and 1:1 for organisations that produce excisable goods.

[426] The rules do not apply to banks, insurance organisations and organisations for which the amount of rent (lease payments) received in the tax period exceeds 50% of the total revenue from the sale of goods (works, services), property rights and income from operations on leasing of property.

[427] Thin capitalisation rules apply to costs (expenses) related to 'controlled debt' to: (a) the founder who directly and (or) indirectly owns at least 20% of the shares of an organisation, and other related persons; (b) interdependent person of the founder (participant) of the Belarusian organisation (provided that the status of interdependent person on the last day of the relevant tax period is maintained) the organisation.

[428] The rules apply to 'controlled debt' which includes any debt under: (a) borrowed funds on loans and borrowings (except for commercial loans); (b) penalties (fines), amounts payable as a result of the application of other measures of liability; and (c) certain types of services (engineering, marketing, consulting, management services, etc.); (d) obligations incurred in connection with the performance of the guarantee obligation to repay debts of the Belarusian organisation for these services.

4.9 Transfer Pricing

[429] Income tax payable depends not only on the actual transaction price stated in the transaction documents. In some cases, when calculating and paying income tax, business entities are required to apply prices corresponding to the existing range of market prices, and in case of any discrepancy, the tax base and, consequently, the tax amount must be corrected by the taxpayer (or will be corrected by a controlling agency during inspection).

[430] The table below describes all types of transactions subject to control in 2023:

Transaction Type	Sum Limits
Foreign trade transactions with an interdependent person	EUR130 000
Transaction on sale or purchase of goods (works, services), property rights made *with the interdependent legal entity – tax resident of Belarus, which does not calculate and does not pay income tax* (exempt from tax) in the calendar year in which the transaction was made. Such persons include:	(excluding VAT and excise duties) – for the organisation, which is not included in the list of large taxpayers;

Transaction Type	*Sum Limits*
– residents of free economic zones; – taxpayers, who apply special tax regimes; – taxpayers carrying out activities in the territories defined by legislative acts, residents of the HTP, the special tourist and recreational park «Augustow canal», Great Stone Industrial Park.	EUR660 000 (excluding VAT and excise duties) – for an organisation included in the list of large tax-payers.
Transaction made with an interdependent person, a taxpayer applying special tax regimes, on the sale or acquisition of – *immovable property* (its part), including transactions resulting in the transfer of residential and (or) non-residential premises to the shareholder of an object of shared construction, the owner of housing bonds; – *housing bonds* in the process of their circulation (except for operations of issuers with bonds of their own issue), performed after the state registration of creation of the object of construction.	None
Foreign trade transactions for the sale or purchase of strategic goods on the list determined by the Council of Ministers of Belarus.	EUR660 000 (excluding VAT, excise tax).

Transactions with an interdependent person are treated as such:
 	
(1) the totality of transactions concluded with the participation (through the mediation) of a third party, which is not interdependent, provided that such person:
  – does not perform significant functions in this set of transactions, except for the organisation of the sale and (or) the acquisition of goods (works, services), property rights by one person to another person recognised as interdependent with this person;
  – does not use any assets and (or) does not take risks to organise the sale and (or) the purchase of goods (works, services), property rights by one person to another person recognised as interdependent with this person.
	None

Transaction Type	Sum Limits
(2) transaction on sale or purchase of goods (works, services), property rights with a resident of an off-shore zone.	EUR130 000 (excluding VAT, excise taxes).

5 EMPLOYMENT CONSIDERATIONS

5.1 Legislative Framework

[431] The sphere of employment relations is basically regulated by the Labour Code of Belarus No. 296-Z dated 26 July 1999 (Labour Code). Also, many other acts of legislation elaborate on more specific issues.

[432] According to the Labour Code, an employment agreement must be concluded in writing. Certain mandatory conditions that must be included in each employment agreement are also stipulated by the Labour Code.

[433] Terms and conditions of an employment agreement that worsen the position of an employee in comparison with legislation and relevant collective agreements are invalid.

[434] The Ministry of Labour and Social Protection of Belarus is the supreme state authority responsible for public policy on labour and employment.

[435] Relations among employees and relations between employees and the employer are also regulated by local legal acts. According to Article 1 of the Labour Code, local legal acts include collective contracts, agreements, internal labour regulations and other acts of a particular employer, adopted according to the established procedure and regulating labour and associated relations.

[436] For example, local legal acts regulating labour routine are provided for in Article 194 of the Labour Code:

- rules for internal labour order, collective contracts/agreements, internal labour regulations and other local legal acts;
- staff schedules;
- employees' job descriptions;
- work schedules (shift schedules);
- leave schedules.

[437] According to the labour legislation and other laws of Belarus, business entities (irrespective of types of activities carried out) must maintain labour protection documentation.

[438] Labour legislation establishes that local legal acts must not aggravate employees' work conditions as prescribed by labour laws and other laws of Belarus regulating relations in the social/labour sphere.

[439] In order to comply with legislative requirements and to avoid conflicts with employees, each employer must always thoroughly elaborate on all aspects of labour and associated relations by means of preparing and approving respective local legal acts.

5.2 Employment Protection

5.2.1 Continuity on Business Transfers

[440] Generally, upon change of control over the business entity, all employment agreements concluded between the business entity and its employees stay in force on the same terms. As a general rule, the acquirer of a business is not able to pre-select the employees it wishes to keep and those it wishes to terminate relations with.

[441] When the owner of the Unitary Enterprise changes, the new owner has the right to terminate the employment agreements with the director, his deputies and the chief accountant not later than three months from the date of acquisition of the ownership right.

[442] According to Article 259 of the Labour Code, an employment contract concluded with the director of the business entity can provide for the possibility of the director's dismissal by virtue of the decision of the sole shareholder or general meeting of the business entity without any culpable grounds, subject to the payment of compensation for early termination in the amount determined by the employment agreement.

5.2.2 Employees Representation

[443] The charter of a business entity may provide for inclusion of a representative of the employees and (or) of a trade union in its board of directors, but there is no such requirement at the legislative level. The sole director (or the chairman of the directorate) cannot be a member of the board of directors.

[444] Under Belarusian legislation, a business entity has no obligation to notify or consult the employees of trade unions on a transfer of shares or the sale of the business. Hence, the employees cannot block or delay such a transaction. Meanwhile, in case of reorganisation of a business entity, continuation of labour relations is carried out with the consent of the employee only.

[445] Trade unions represent the interests of employees in collective negotiations, conclusion of a collective bargaining agreement and control over its implementation, etc. Trade unions also have the right, upon the request of their members and other citizens, to apply to the court with a statement of claim in defence of their labour and socio-economic rights and interests.

[446] At the moment, the creation of trade unions in business entities is not compulsory. In private business entities, trade unions are rare.

[447] If a trade union is established in a business entity, the following notification rules are applicable. In cases stipulated by Belarusian legislation, termination of an employment contract on the initiative of the employer can be made only two weeks prior to notification of the trade union. In cases stipulated by collective agreements, termination of an employment contract on the initiative of the employer may be carried out only with the prior consent of the trade union.

[448] Liquidation or reorganisation of a business entity, its branch, full or partial suspension of production on the initiative of the employer entailing job cuts or a worsening in working conditions, can be carried out only three months prior to notification of the trade union and negotiations conducted on the observance of the rights and interests of employees.

5.2.3 Termination

[449] Termination of individual employment agreements is possible only on limited grounds set out by the legislation. The employer cannot determine additional grounds for termination of the employment relations that are not provided for by law.

[450] As a general rule, any employment agreement can be terminated at any time upon mutual agreement of the parties, except cases, provided by law for a certain group of employees. The common grounds for termination of employment relations with employees in Belarus are as follows:

- mutual agreement of the parties;
- expiration of the fixed-term employment agreement;
- termination of the employment agreement by the initiative or on demand of the employee, or by the initiative of the employer;
- transfer of an employee to another employer or transition to an elective position of an officer;
- refusal of the employee to continue the employment relationship in connection with:
- transfer to another employer;
- amendment of essential terms of the employment;
- reorganisation of the company;
- circumstances beyond the control of the parties;
- termination of employment agreement with a probation period.

[451] A fixed-term employment agreement terminates on the expiration of its term. If, upon the expiration of the term of a fixed-term employment agreement, the employment relationship actually continues and none of the parties has demanded its termination, then the employment agreement is deemed to continue for an indefinite period.

[452] An employee has the right to unilaterally terminate an employment agreement concluded for an indefinite period on one month's prior notice. An employee also has the right to demand the termination of the fixed-term employment agreement in the following cases:

– the presence of circumstances that exclude or significantly complicate the continuation of work (the employee's health status, retirement age, radioactive contamination of the territory and other cases);

– violation by the employer of the employment contract, collective bargaining agreement or labour legislation.

[453] Any employment agreement can be terminated by the employer in the following cases:

(a) liquidation of a business entity, its branch, or downsizing;

(b) inconsistency of the employee with the position held due to his/her state of health, or insufficient qualifications preventing the continuation of work;

(c) systematic non-fulfilment of duties by the employee without any good reason, if disciplinary measures were previously applied to the employee;

(d) failure to appear for work for more than four months in a row due to temporary disability (excluding maternity leave). For employees who have lost their ability to work due to work injury or disease, the position is retained pending vocational rehabilitation or recovery from the disability;

(e) a single gross violation by an employee of labour duties including:

    (1) truancy (absence from work for more than three hours during a working day without any good reason) or absence from work in connection with serving an administrative arrest that impedes the performance of labour duties;

    (2) appearing at work in a state of alcoholic, narcotic or toxic intoxication, as well as drinking alcoholic beverages, using drugs, psychotropic or toxic substances during working hours or at the place of work;

    (3) committing theft of the property of the employer at the place of work;

    (4) violation of technological, executive or labour discipline, which caused damage to the organisation in an amount exceeding three accrued average monthly wages of employees of the Republic of Belarus;

    (5) forcing employees to participate in a strike, creating obstacles for other employees to perform their job duties, calling on workers to stop performing their job duties without good reason;

    (6) participation of an employee in an illegal strike, as well as in other forms of refusal of an employee to perform work duties (in whole or in part) without good reason;

    (7) a gross violation of labour protection requirements, resulting in injury or death of other employees.

(f) infliction of property damage to the state, legal entities and (or) individuals, established by an entered-into-force court decision by the employee in connection with the performance of labour duties;

(g) repeated (two or more times within six months) violation of the legislatively established procedure for considering applications from citizens and legal entities;

(h) repeated (two or more times within six months) submission of incomplete or inaccurate information to the authorised bodies.

[454] Moreover, an employment contract is subject to termination for the following circumstances beyond the control of the parties:

- conscription of an employee for military service;
- reinstatement at work of an employee who previously carried out the relevant work;
- violation of the established rules for hiring;
- non-election to the position (including by competition);
- punishment of an employee under a court verdict excluding the continuation of work;
- death of an employee;
- establishment of restrictions on engaging in certain types of activities, preventing the continuation of work;
- transfer of an employee, with their consent, to another employer or transfer to an elective position.

5.2.4 Labour Costs

[455] Business entities and IEs are free to independently determine wage conditions taking due account the complexity of the work, skills of employees, working conditions, etc.

[456] The Unified Wage Scale of Belarus may be applied in establishing wage conditions, though its application is not obligatory. Hence, business entities have the right to choose any system of wage payment, either applying the Unified Wage Scale or not. Business entities normally pay wages to their employees on the basis of local legal acts adopted by them.

[457] The minimum monthly wage is determined by the government (BYN554 or ca. EUR185, as of April 2023); however, the maximum wage amount is not limited. Wage costs are included in production and sale expenses and are also accounted for in price formation and taxation procedures.

[458] Nominal accrued average wage of employees in Belarus in January 2023 amounted to BYN1 685 (USD632).

5.2.5 Working Conditions

[459] A working pattern is a manner of distribution of norms of daily and weekly working and rest hours during day, week, month and other calendar periods by an employer for its employees.

[460] A working pattern for the employees is developed on the basis of the schedule of work applicable by the employer and is determined by the internal work regulations or by the operating schedule (shift schedule).

[461] Standard working time cannot exceed forty hours a week. For some categories of employees, reduced working time is established. The working week has five or six working days, and Sunday is a general day off. Normally, a working day comprises eight working hours with a one-hour lunch break. There are specific norms that regulate night work, work on weekends and holidays, employment of minors, etc.

[462] Employers are obliged to provide all guarantees and compensations for work on weekends/holidays and during night time as stipulated for employees by the labour legislation. Any overtime work must be compensated (by additional payment or by providing an additional unpaid day of rest).

[463] Employees are entitled to annual labour (basic and additional) and social leaves by virtue of grounds stipulated by the Labour Code. During such leaves, an average salary (so-called vacation allowance) must be saved for the employee calculated in a manner established by legislation.

[464] The minimum period of basic annual labour leave is twenty-four days. Employment agreement cannot contain provisions aggravating employees' working conditions (as prescribed by law), and any employment agreement will be deemed invalid if less than twenty-four days of basic annual labour leave is specified by it.

[465] The following public holidays are non-work days in Belarus:

- 1 and 2 January – New Year;
- 7 January – Orthodox Christmas;
- 8 March – Women's Day;
- according to the Orthodox calendar (on Tuesday on the second week after Easter) – Radunitsa;
- 1 May – Labour Day;
- 9 May – Victory Day;
- 3 July – Independence Day of Belarus (the National Holiday);
- 7 November – Day of the October Revolution;
- 25 December – Catholic Christmas.

5.3 Pensions

[466] There is a compulsory state insurance system in Belarus which includes:

- pension insurance for cases when the insured person reaches retirement age, disability and loss of the breadwinner;
- social insurance for cases of temporary disability, pregnancy and childbirth, caring for a child under the age of 3, caring for a disabled child under the age of 18, death of a person or a member of their family.

[467] The Social Security Fund is formed from contributions that are charged on salaries payable to employees. Thirty-four per cent of an employee's salary is paid by the employer, and one per cent is paid by the employer for the employee.

[468] When calculating contributions, a benefit is applicable to employees of residents of the HTP, employees of residents of the Great Stone Industrial Park, a joint company for the development of this park, employees of the OJSC 'Chinese-Belarusian Investment Fund' and the CJSC 'Management Company of the Chinese-Belarusian Investment Fund'. The benefit means that compulsory insurance contributions are charged only on that part of employees' payments equating to 1 average salary in the state (in January 2023 1 average salary in the state amounted to BYN1 685 (USD632). The employee may refuse to apply for this benefit.

5.4 Retention of Key Management and Employees

[469] In order to minimise the risk of key employees leaving after the transaction, the expiration dates of employment contracts concluded with them are normally checked within the due diligence exercise. A condition precedent to the closing of M&A transaction may include the conclusion or prolongation by the target business entity of fixed-term employment contracts with the key employees.

[470] If the key employees are shareholders of the target business entity, then the transaction documents can provide their obligation to devote sufficient time to the business entity's activities. If one of the parties to the transaction documents is the HTP resident, the parties can include non-solicitation and non-compete clauses in agreements.

[471] From 28 April 2021, amendments to the Law 'On Companies' came into force which provide for the possibility to transfer shares in the statutory fund to the employees of business entities free of charge. The nature of this rule is similar to the institution of the employee option.

5.5 Treatment of Foreign Employees

5.5.1 Permission for Labour Activity

[472] From 1 July 2023, a new edition of the Law 'On external labour migration' comes into force in Belarus, and the regulation in the field of treatment of foreign employees is significantly changed. All features of labour relations with foreigners are described taking into account these legislative amendments.

[473] In Belarus, business entities may attract and hire foreign employees, including director positions. Foreigners having no permission for permanent residence in the territory of Belarus have the right to labour activity once they have obtained a special employment permit and have concluded an employment contract.

[474] An employment agreement concluded with a foreigner having no permission for permanent residence in Belarus must contain additional conditions as follows:

- salary not less than the minimum salary required in Belarus on the date of conclusion of the employment contract;
- conditions of resettlement in Belarus, medical service, catering and lodging in Belarus.

[475] An employment agreement must be concluded in written form in the Russian and/or Belarusian language. Where a foreign employee lacks knowledge of Russian or Belarusian, an employment contract must also be concluded in their native language or in another language known to such employee.

[476] A special permit is granted to employers in respect of their foreign employees for one year. Special permits are granted for two years with respect to highly skilled employees simultaneously conforming to the two following conditions:

- a high level of professional knowledge, skills and expertise confirmed by academic credentials and employment experience in the same occupation for at least five years;
- monthly remuneration exceeds five times the amount of the minimum monthly emolument required in Belarus.

[477] There is no need to receive a special permit for foreign employees who:

- have a permission for permanent residence in Belarus;
- are being employed according to another procedure provided for by an international agreement of Belarus (e.g., citizens of the Russian Federation, the Republic of Kazakhstan, the Republic of Armenia, the Kyrgyz Republic who are excluded from regulation on the intake and usage of foreign labour force);
- are employed as chief executives of foreign entities' representative offices;
- have graduated from a technical, secondary specialised or higher education institution in Belarus and are employed according to their degree and qualification;
- are employed by an HTP resident;
- are winners (awardees) of national/international competitions or have been specially acknowledged for their professional activities in case of their employment in a specialty that is part of the scope of their professional activities, where they have been winners (awardees) or have been specially acknowledged and etc.

[478] citizens having no permission for permanent residence in Belarus can seek employment by themselves or with the assistance of business entities, IEs or foreign organisations that render recruitment services.

[479] Belarusian citizens and foreign citizens permanently residing in Belarus have a priority right to employment.

[480] Until 1 July 2023, a Belarusian entity that employs more than ten foreigners having no permission for permanent residence in Belarus was obliged to obtain permission for employment of foreign labour force. With the entry into force of the new edition of the Law 'On external labour migration' this requirement has been eliminated.

5.5.2 Entry into the Territory of Belarus for Labour Activities

[481] As a general rule, foreigners may enter the territory of Belarus only after obtaining a Belarusian visa.

[482] There is no requirement for obtaining employment visas for citizens of Azerbaijan, Armenia, Georgia, Kazakhstan, Kyrgyzstan, the Russian Federation, Moldova, Uzbekistan, Tajikistan, Turkmenistan, Ukraine and Ecuador.

[483] Visa-free entry is also provided for citizens of Argentina, Brazil, Venezuela, China, Cuba, Serbia, Israel, Qatar, Macedonia, Mongolia, United Arab Emirates, Turkey and Montenegro. From 15 April 2022 to 31 December 2023, a visa-free entry is also valid for citizens of Lithuania, Latvia (as well as persons with the status of a non-citizen of Latvia). Also, from 1 July 2022 to 31 December 2023, a visa-free entry was introduced for citizens of Poland. However, if citizens of these countries are planning to carry out labour, commercial or other income-generating activities in Belarus, they are obliged to obtain a visa in advance.

[484] Also, citizens of seventy-six states, as listed in the annexe to Presidential Edict No. 8 dated 9 January 2017, are entitled to visa-free entry/departure in/from Belarus through the Minsk National Airport, Brest, Vitebsk, Gomel, Grodno, Mogilev airport border stations for not more than thirty days (without any additional registration with Belarusian migration authorities). Almost all EU countries, the USA, Japan and other states are on the list. These measures are targeted at spurring travels by foreign businessmen, investors, tourists and individuals to Belarus.

[485] All foreigners arriving in Belarus must within ten days (except for Sundays and public holidays) register themselves at a local registration authority according to their place of stay or at the single electronic services portal portal.gov.by. When accommodating themselves in a hotel, hostel, health spa or other collective places of residence, foreigners are registered by administrative bodies of such institutions by default during the check-in procedure.

[486] As of 28 March 2018, the following categories of persons are entitled to visa-free entry in Belarus (using the special entry procedure):

- persons engaged by HTP residents for labour activities under employment contracts;
- persons who are property holders, founders, participants/shareholders of HTP residents and their employees.

[487] The same procedure applies to the residents of the Great Stone Industrial Park.

[488] In order to carry out labour activities in Belarus, a foreigner may obtain one of the following types of entry visas:

(1) *C (short-term 'employment' visa):* which is issued on the basis of one of the following documents:

(a) a copy of a special permit for labour activity in Belarus for a foreigner notarised by a Belarusian notary (hereinafter – the special permit);

(b) a notification made by a local citizenship and migration office of issuing a special permit to a foreigner delivered to a foreign establishment through the channels of departmental electronic mail of the Ministry of Foreign Affairs (hereinafter – the MFA);

(c) permission to open a representative office or its notarised copy and a letter from a foreign organisation on the appointment of a foreigner as the head of the representative office – for issuing an entry visa to the head of the representative office of a foreign organisation.

(2) *D (long-term 'employment' visa):* which is issued to citizens of migration-friendly states on the basis of an original petition of a Belarusian business entity or of a representative office of a foreign business entity in Belarus (including banks) and one of the following documents:

(a) a copy of the special permit certified by a Belarusian notary (or information available in the foreign institution on the issuance of a special permit to a foreigner for the right to engage an immigrant employee in labour activity in Belarus);

(b) an application for a visa issued by a legal entity of the Republic of Belarus or a representative office of a foreign organisation.

(3) *D long-term visa (business contacts):* which is issued to maintain business relations on the basis of documents of a legal entity of the Republic of Belarus (including constituent documents) confirming that the foreigner is the founder of a commercial organisation in Belarus. This visa may also be obtained by foreigners working in a representative office of a foreign organisation as well as representative offices of this foreign organisation in third countries or founders and employees of a foreign organisation which has established the specified representative office.

[489] A foreigner can enter Belarus having any other visa provided that such foreigner obtains a multiple exit-entry visa from a local citizenship and migration office (providing such foreigner has a temporary residence permit).

Entry visas are issued by diplomatic missions and consular offices of Belarus. Exit-entry visas are issued by local citizenship and migration offices according to the place of a foreigner's residence in Belarus.

[490] Citizens of states having no diplomatic missions or consular offices in Belarus must apply for a visa to the General Consular Department of the MFA and border control authorities of Belarus.

5.5.3 Stay in the Territory of Belarus

[491] All foreigners arriving in Belarus must be registered according to their actual place of residence at the local authority of internal affairs within ten calendar days (except for Sundays and holidays).

[492] International agreements of Belarus can provide longer terms of stay in Belarus without registration by the internal affairs bodies for certain categories of foreigners.

[493] For example, citizens of Lithuania, Latvia, Ukraine, the Republic of Armenia and the Republic of Kazakhstan may stay in the territory of Belarus without registration for thirty days from the day of entry, and citizens of the Russian Federation – for ninety days from the day of entry. Citizens of the Kyrgyz Republic and members of their families may also stay in Belarus without registration for thirty days from the date of entry, provided they conclude an employment or a civil contract within five days from the date of entry. If they stay in the territory of Belarus for more than thirty days, they have to register according to their place of residence at the local authority of internal affairs under the standard procedure.

[494] Foreigners can stay temporarily, reside temporarily or reside permanently in the territory of Belarus.

[495] All foreigners in the territory of Belarus having no permission for temporary or permanent residence are subject to the rules of the Temporary Stay Regime in Belarus. The total term of a foreigner's temporary stay in Belarus depends on the validity term of their visa and cannot exceed ninety days in a year.

[496] International agreements of Belarus may provide longer terms of temporary stay in Belarus without obtaining permission for temporary or permanent residence for certain categories of foreigners.

[497] If a foreigner intends to stay in Belarus for more than ninety days in a year (or longer than the term determined by the relevant international agreement), such foreigner will have to obtain permission for temporary or permanent residence.

[498] A permission for temporary residence is issued to foreigners who have entered Belarus for certain purposes, including labour, business or other activities. Decisions on granting such permission are made by the local internal affairs body according to such foreigner's place of stay.

[499] A permission for permanent residence gives a foreigner the right to permanent residence in Belarus. It is issued by the Ministry of Internal Affairs or other authorities of internal affairs for certain categories of foreigners determined by the legislation of Belarus.

6 ACCOUNTING TREATMENT

[500] The main accounting requirements are established in the Law of Belarus 'On Accounting and Reporting'. The recommendations of the supervisory authorities also apply (the Council of Ministers, the Ministry of Finance, etc.).

[501] The organisations in Belarus are required to perform accounting in accordance with National Accounting and Reporting Standards (NARS).

As the rule, the socially significant organisations (OJSCs that are the founders of UEs and (or) the main economic companies in relation to subsidiaries of economic companies (OJSC), banks and non-bank credit and financial organisations, insurance organisations, joint-stock investment funds) are required to apply International Finance Reporting Standards (IFRS) when preparing financial statements.

For the period 2022–2024, certain socially significant organisations have the right not to provide consolidated financial statements, including those in accordance with IFRS.

[502] Annual and interim financial statements (with the exception of monthly financial statements) of commercial organisations consist of the following forms:

- balance sheet;
- income statement;
- statement of changes in equity;
- cash-flow statement;
- notes to the accounting statement.

[503] Expenses related to the reorganisation are accounted for as a part of non-operating expenses and are reflected in the corresponding reporting period in the accounting records of the organisation incurring these expenses as other expenses from operations that are not directly related to production and sales.

[504] In the case of acquisitions for accounting purposes, neither profits nor losses of the target organisation contribute to the amount of profit of the acquiring company. Losses in such a situation affect the amount of retained earnings (uncovered loss) of the acquiring company.

[505] Intangible assets are recognised if, among other things, the organisation expects to receive economic benefits from the use of such assets and may restrict the access of others to these benefits and the initial cost of the assets can be reliably determined. Generally, intangible assets are subject to amortisation, but in particular cases, the organisation has the right to revalue intangible assets at the current market value at the end of the reporting period.

[506] Consolidated financial statements are accounting statements prepared for a group of organisations as accounting statements of a single organisation. Consolidated financial statements as the financial statements of a single organisation are made by a group of organisations:

- a holding company;
- a business company and its UEs, subsidiaries and dependent business companies;
- a UE and its subsidiaries. The procedure and deadlines for submitting consolidated financial statements are established by the owner of the property (founders, participants) of the organisation and other persons authorised to receive consolidated financial statements by the legislation of Belarus or the constituent documents of such organisation.

[507] Organisations that are united in a group of organisations must apply the same accounting methods in the reporting periods for which the consolidated financial statements are prepared.

[508] Consolidated financial statements are prepared by the parent company according to the forms established by it independently.

[509] Goodwill for accounting purposes is listed as an asset only for the consolidated financial statements. According to the national standard, goodwill is recognised as an asset that arises on the acquisition date in the amount of the excess of the value of the parent company's long-term financial investments in the authorised capital of the subsidiary or associates over the value of the parent company's share of the equity of the subsidiary or associate.

[510] The amount of goodwill incurred on the acquisition date (excluding the value of trademarks and service marks incurred on the acquisition date) is recorded as a separate item in non-current assets.

7 FUTURE DEVELOPMENTS

[511] From 2017 to 2020, Belarusian legislation has become more and more flexible and adapted to the needs of foreign investors. A big breakthrough was Decree No. 8 adopted in 2017. The decree allowed HTP residents to use the tools of English law, which are often used for structuring M&A transactions and regulating of corporate rights of investors and founders. For example, options, convertible loans, indemnities, irrevocable powers of attorney.

[512] However, gradually the scope of their application has expanded outside the HTP. The Great Stone Industrial Park has followed the example of the HTP. On 11 June 2021, legislative changes were adopted allowing the residents of the Great Stone Industrial Park and a number of entities operating on its territory to use such instruments of English law as convertible loans and option agreements.

Outside the HTP and Great Stone Industrial Park, business entities have also been granted the opportunity to implement mentioned instruments. The Law 'On Companies' enshrines the possibility of granting options to employees, the possibility of a convertible loan and certain other instruments for any business entity. On 9 July 2021, a new version of the Law of Belarus 'On Currency Regulation and Currency Control' came into force which requires currency agreements concluded by residents of Belarus with non-residents to be registered on a special portal (however, not all agreements with non-residents are subject to registration but those meeting certain criteria).

[513] The Belarusian legislation is becoming more and more open to new corporate and other instruments that regulate the relationship between founders and investors. It is expected that those instruments existing within special regimes only (the HTP and Great Stone Industrial Park) and not yet available for other business

entities, will be implemented in the legislation through analogues based on Belarusian law. Although many classic instruments of M&A transactions have been implemented in the Belarusian legislation, judicial practice on the use of such instruments has not yet been fully formed and is expected to develop, showing the peculiarities of structuring M&A transactions under Belarusian law using the implemented instruments and their analogues based on Belarusian law.